EARLY MAN
Prehistory and the
Civilizations of the Ancient Near East

EARLY MAN

Prehistory and the Civilizations of the Ancient Near East

CHESTER G. STARR

Professor of Ancient History, University of Michigan

New York
OXFORD UNIVERSITY PRESS
London 1973 Toronto

PREFACE

This book, together with *The Ancient Greeks* and *The Ancient Romans*, reflects the influence of two historians, who worked in very different ways. One is R. M. Schedel, sometime teacher of history in the Bloomington (Illinois) High School, whose dedication to his subject inspired me to be a historian. The other man, likewise from Illinois, is James Henry Breasted, who became a world-famous scholar of ancient Egypt and the founder of the Oriental Institute. In 1916 Breasted published a general survey of ancient history, *Ancient Times*, which was my first introduction to this fascinating subject as it has been to many others.

Today there is a need for a new general exploration of the earliest stages of human history down to the fall of the Roman empire. In the first place archeological and other investigations have revolutionized our understanding of prehistory, of early Egypt and Mesopotamia, and even in some respects of Greece and Rome. In the second place the questions which we would ask about our past are very different from those of half a century ago; for the world in which we live has changed markedly. History, after all, is an account of the past which helps us to understand ourselves in the present.

In these three short books it has not been my aim to tell everything; in that case they could not have been short. Rather, I have sought to stress the most important aspects of human development over the past million years so as to encourage the reader's imagination and curiosity. The brief bibliographies suggest interesting works which give detailed information on those aspects about which one wishes to know more.

To list all the people who have helped me by reading the text, by answering questions, or above all by providing photographs would take a great deal of space. The illustration of these works, incidentally, has been as time-consuming a task as writing the text; for the pictures are intended to reinforce and also to enlarge the story as told in the printed words. Let me simply express my gratitude for all the assistance which I have received. Above all I hope that the reader of this work or its two successors will find the early history of mankind as absorbing and as illuminating as it has been to the author.

Chester G. Starr

ANN ARBOR, MICHIGAN
December 1972

CONTENTS

PART II   **The Origins of Civilization**

PART III   Empires and Subjects

* *

PART I

On the Track of Early Man

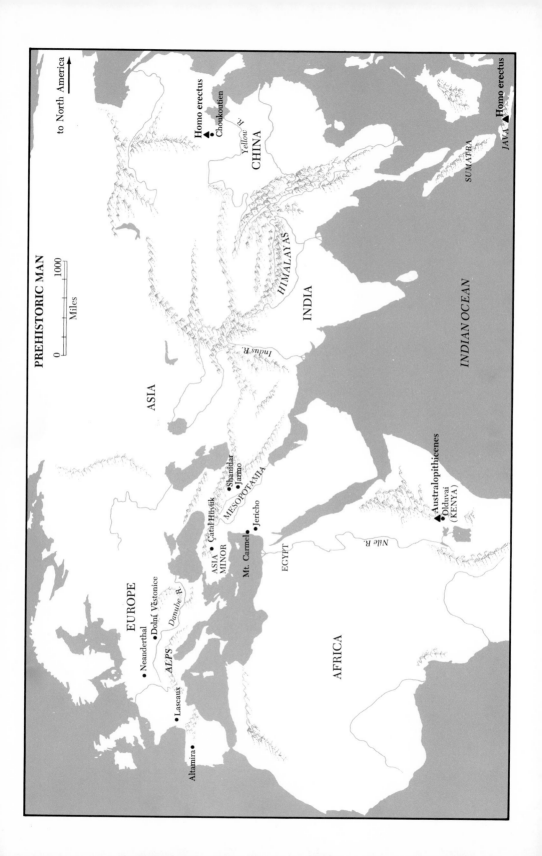

PREHISTORIC MAN

to North America

0   1000
Miles

EUROPE
Neanderthal •
Dolní Věstonice •
Danube R.
ALPS
Altamira •
Lascaux •

ASIA

ASIA MINOR
Çatal Hüyük •
Mt. Carmel •
Jericho •
MESOPOTAMIA
Shanidar •
Jarmo •
Indus R.
HIMALAYAS
INDIA
CHINA
Yellow R.
Homo erectus ▲ • Choukoutien

SUMATRA
JAVA ▲ Homo erectus

INDIAN OCEAN

EGYPT
Nile R.
AFRICA
Australopithicenes ▲ • Olduvai (KENYA)

History is one of the main ways in which men come closer to understanding their own nature. Its particular method is to study what men have done in time and space. This survey requires "facts and dates," as history is sometimes described; but the historian uses such specific information primarily to help prove and illuminate a general view about the nature of man.

In the study of the earliest stages of human development we shall find that facts and dates are not easily discovered. Even so, it is worth looking at early man for at least three reasons. In the first place, the story illustrates the inherent possibilities and diversities of human achievements. Secondly, we ourselves owe more to these distant ancestors than we may realize. Apart from our body structure itself, what we might consider purely instinctive reactions in matters of food, sexual behavior, family structure, or fears of the unknown have actually been shaped by the many generations of earlier human development. Thirdly, the tale may be comforting in a time when modern pessimists fear that we may not last out the next 50 years, for our prehistoric forebears carried on for hundreds of thousands of years in the most difficult conditions.

For most of this period human progress was almost imperceptible, and only in relatively recent times have we advanced more and more swiftly. Yet our ancestors had certain inherent strengths and skills which enabled them to survive, even on a very simple level, and to reproduce their species for many thousands of generations. What were these strengths? and why did it take so long for mankind to be able to change its ways of life more rapidly?

Part I of this book will take up in chronological order the first two stages of man's existence, the food-gathering period and then the beginnings of food-raising. This part will be much the largest section, for it took mankind an extremely long time to reach the level of civilization. Also we need to explore very carefully how the historian knows—and how he guesses from his evidence—almost as much as to read the picture of prehistory which he gives.

Parts II and III will be devoted to two major stages of civilization in the Near East. Here one cannot hope to survey all aspects of human development, for once civilization begins the information available to the historian is much more extensive. In Part II we shall visit one of the first civilized societies which can be seen clearly, Babylon in the days of king Hammurapi (about 1750 B.C.). Then, after a big jump, Part III will sketch the consolidation of the Near East in the great Persian empire (about 500 B.C.).

At the beginning we must travel widely over much of Asia, Africa, and Europe. Thereafter the scene will be mainly the ancient Near East and its Mediterranean shores, down to 500 B.C. Whether complex or simple, the achievements of our ancestors are as exciting as the development of a helpless, new-born baby into a mature, self-confident adult.

Years B.C.		
	Food-Gathering Peoples	
1,000,000 and before	Australopithicenes	
400,000	**Homo erectus**	
110,000	Neanderthal man	
35,000	**Homo sapiens**	
28,000	Beginning of cave painting	
10,000	Retreat of glaciers	
	Food-Raising Era	
8,000	Essentially modern climate	
7,000	Agricultural villages in Near East	
	Civilization	
Just before 3,000	Cities in Mesopotamia Kingdom of Egypt	

CHAPTER 1

The Earliest Food-Gatherers

The Search for Early Man ❀❀❀❀❀❀❀❀❀❀❀❀❀❀❀❀❀❀❀❀❀
Usually history is described as an account of man's past based on written documents. Since writing is a product of civilization, everything before about 3000 B.C. is "prehistory," which rests solely on physical remains. Objects such as flint tools have long been known, but down through the 18th century they were called thunder-stones. There was little concept that mankind could have had a long past. Indeed a prominent English scholar, Archbishop Ussher, calculated from the Biblical account that man was created in 4004 B.C.

In the 19th century geologists began to be ever more aware of the tremendously long span of time involved in the earth's history. Charles Darwin published in 1859 a very influential book, *On the Origin of Species,* suggesting that living creatures were products of natural selection over a long period, though Darwin himself did not make any serious comments about man's evolution in this book.

By this date a French customs official, Jacques Boucher de Perthes, had already been roaming up and down the Somme river valley for more than two decades in a search for prehistoric flints. The diggers whom Boucher de Perthes hired took a human jawbone from a modern cemetery at one point and secretly placed it in a prehistoric level for him to find; but even so the French enthusiast uncovered a great deal of solid evidence. What he established was that stone tools appeared in the same layers with extinct species of animals. Mankind, in other words, must have had a long past.

This imprint of the left foot of a Neanderthal man was found on the floor of an Italian cave. It is the only surviving evidence of early human bodies, as distinguished from their bones.

Across the past hundred years the antiquity of man has become an accepted idea. The terms Paleolithic (for the era which is called in this book the "food-gathering" stage) and Neolithic (here called "food-raising") were coined in 1863, and the search for early man has absorbed the lives of many dedicated scholars. Any survey of prehistoric development must also be in large part a story of *how* our knowledge has been expanded. Sometimes it is a tale of accidental and happy finds; more often nowadays there is first-rate detective work, combined with a great deal of very hard labor.

The archeologists who dig up the past may start at times with bulldozers, but eventually they are on their hands and knees with dental picks and toothbrushes. Poor food and dysentery, angry rhinoceroses which must be shot, uncivilized tribes which do not appreciate outsiders poking about in their mountains—all these have at one point or another been an added burden to an archeologist. Then, when scholars have made their discoveries, they have repeatedly had to face the skepticism or hostility of their colleagues as to the meaning of the finds. The idea, for example, that mankind had existed in North America more than 4000 years ago was ruthlessly and rather successfully opposed by one eminent scholar for almost a generation.

Excavation at Shanidar cave (see p. 17). Just beyond the bucket hoist a paleontologist is starting to clean the bones of Shanidar IV; the upper archeologist is at the point where another skeleton was found.

Ralph S. Solecki

A Note of Caution ❀❀❀❀❀❀❀❀❀❀❀❀❀❀❀❀❀❀❀❀❀❀❀❀❀❀
Today we *think* that we can trace the main stages of early human life with some accuracy. These stages are listed in Time Chart No. 1 and are discussed in the following sections. For each successive stage there is more information than for the one before, but always in the study of early man important questions may come to our minds which simply cannot be answered. When the evidence is limited, it is better to admit that limit than to conceal our ignorance by making up theories. Some poorly grounded but popular speculations will be noted as the story develops, for a student of history needs to have a healthy amount of skepticism. Even so, the knowledge about a very distant past which has been built up in a century is remarkable.

Another reason for being cautious is the fact that our views of the subject are always changing as the evidence increases. In the newspapers tomorrow there may be a report of a new find which significantly alters the picture, particularly with regard to the physical development of mankind. As applied to human alterations, the theory of evolution by slow changes (and occasional mutations) seems a sensible one, but unfortunately a tidy series of evolutionary steps has not yet been demonstrated to prove the theory in all its details. The historian can only take on faith the proposition that men developed, somehow or other, out of the Primate family of mammals; and the genetic relations among the four stages of men we shall look at are far from clear.

The Australopithecines ●●●●●●●●●●●●●●●●●●●●●●●●●●●●
The earliest link in the evolutionary chain of man himself is also the latest which has been discovered. In the southern half of Africa, reaching up into Kenya, several varieties of Australopithecines were running around apparently as many as 5½ million years ago.* They stood about 4 feet high and weighed sometimes a bit over 100 pounds; their cranial volume ranged between 450 and 750 cc., averaging 576 cc. (modern gorillas average just under 500 cc.). Their body structure shows clearly that they had an essentially upright posture. Whether these Australopithecines made stone tools to chop up their meat, as against simply using bones and other natu-

---

* Australopithecine is pronounced o-strā-lō-pith-e-sīn and is derived from Greek words meaning "southern apelike." The pronunciation of unusual names is given in the Glossary along with probable dates.

ral objects, has been fiercely debated; but a recent report suggests that flakes knocked off in the process of converting pebbles into chopping tools can be dated at about 2½ million years.

The first example of this predecessor of man was the skull of a baby which was given to the South African anatomist Raymond Dart by one of his students in 1924. Thereafter Dart and others prospected for more bones, and in the next 20 years discovered enough evidence to suggest that there were several types of Australopithecines. Another devoted student has been Louis S. B. Leakey, the son of a missionary in Kenya and the only white man ever initiated into the native Kikuyu tribe. Leakey was excited at the age of 13 by reading a book about prehistoric Britain and decided to find early man in eastern Africa. Despite a limited educational background he persevered in getting his degree in anthropology at Cambridge University.

Thereafter Leakey spent his life in exploring particularly the Olduvai gorge in Tanzania, a few degrees from the equator. Here geologic processes over the ages have laid down strata in a prehistoric lake which were cut repeatedly by a river, uplifted, and filled again. The result is a miniature Grand Canyon, 300 feet deep and over 15 miles long, which presents at least 5 beds of geological and

Olduvai gorge

Photograph by Hugo Van Lawick, © 1963 National Geographic Society

animal remains stretching over the past 2 million years. At the present time there is almost no water in summer, when the temperature gets up to 110° F., but the excavators have had the company of poisonous snakes and, in wetter months, lions and rhinoceroses.

The results, however, have been worth the discomforts and dangers; for evidence from Australopithecine to modern man has appeared in abundance during the work of Leakey and his students over a generation. Chopping tools have been found in the lowest Bed I, but from the upper half of Bed II on simple hand-axes were made in more and more careful fashion.

Whether Australopithecines lie on the direct course of human evolution remains uncertain. To duck around this problem they are often called hominids (in contrast to "homo" or man proper). Nonetheless they had some of the fundamental physical qualities which have distinguished mankind ever since. For one thing they lived on the ground. To do so they ran (or walked less well) on two feet in an essentially upright position and had at their command a superior nervous and mental capacity, which was evident in a relatively large brain. Their eyes, like ours and those of some apes, were located in such a position that they could focus in stereovision; for mankind sight largely replaces smell and sound as a mode of warning ·and a means of grasping the outside world. Australopithecines did not have the large canine teeth present in monkeys and apes; our ancestors have always relied on a hand in which the thumb could be opposed to the other fingers and could grasp tools as specialized extensions of arm muscles.

If Australopithecines are indeed responsible for the chopping tools which turn up in the Olduvai gorge and elsewhere in southern Africa, they had taken the first steps toward forming a "culture." This term means the development of a way of living and making things which is passed on *socially* rather than by physical inheritance. The strengths of man, which have allowed him to survive and develop, have not been purely physical powers, for many other animals excel here. Much more important for man have been his mental capacity and social culture.

Homo Erectus ❀❀❀❀❀❀❀❀❀❀❀❀❀❀❀❀❀❀❀❀❀❀❀❀❀

While Australopithecines have thus far been discovered only in southern Africa (with one possibility in Asia), the next human stage turned up first in eastern Asia. A young Dutch doctor, Eugène

Dubois, decided late in the 19th century to search for early man and felt a warm climate would be the best place to look. So he went to the Dutch East Indies in the colonial service and investigated first Sumatra, then Java. On the latter island he found in 1891-92 the remains of "Java man," later called *Pithecanthropus erectus* (erect-walking ape-man) and now termed *homo erectus.**

In the 1920's a Canadian scholar teaching anatomy at a Peking medical school, Davidson Black, was given a molar which excited him greatly; in fact he described a new race of man solely on the evidence of this one tooth. Eventually he secured funds to excavate at Choukoutien, 26 miles southwest of Peking. The Chinese called this limestone site Dragon-Bone Hill, because they had long prospected there for ancient bones to grind up for medical prescriptions. Although Black died before the excavations were finished, the remains of over 40 early examples of *homo erectus* were found by him and his successors. During the confusion at the outbreak of World War II the skeletal material was lost, but casts fortunately had been made and they survive.

* Dubois was so upset by the skepticism and arguments over his finds that at one point he actually locked up his evidence and it remained hidden away until his death.

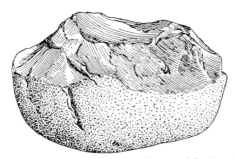

T. P. O'Brien, The Prehistory of the Uganda Protectorate, *fig. 6.*

Among the earliest stone tools of man were chopping tools made from pebbles, as shown above. Below is a broken spear, made of yew and hardened in the fire, which was found in a very early level at Clacton (England). Flint spearheads were not used until late in the hunting age (for an example see p. 29).

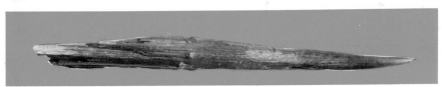

British Museum (Natural History)

Excavation at Choukoutien. The squares on the wall were laid out to permit methodical digging and identification of the location of objects found.

American Museum of Natural History, New York

At Choukoutien, rock falls from the roofs of the shelters, wind-blown dirt, and the garbage of *homo erectus* had built up a deposit at one place more than 160 feet thick. There were bones of saber-toothed tigers and leopards; there were also bones of animals which the human inhabitants had eaten, including elephant, rhinoceros, rabbit, and especially deer.

It is even possible that men ate their fellows; for many skulls turned up by themselves without other parts of the skeleton, in which the base had been deliberately enlarged. Many modern scholars, apparently willing to believe the worst of their ancestors, think that the objective was to get at the brains as a delicacy; others point out that primitive peoples today often revere their departed relatives by preserving their empty skulls. As is often true in pre-history, we have only the evidence and must decide for ourselves what it means. Perhaps the most significant fact about the skulls is that the brain capacity runs from 915 to 1225 cc., averaging 1046 cc.—almost twice that of Australopithecines. *Homo erectus* was also taller, ranging up to about 5 feet.

The tools used by *homo erectus* were made out of greenstone pebbles from a nearby streambed, quartz crystals from hills a few miles away, and also sandstone and chert. Essentially they were chopping tools to hack meat, like those apparently associated with Australopithecine layers in southern Africa, but scrapers and flakes were also found. Over the many thousands of years during which men lived at Choukoutien there was almost no development in the patterns of tool-making. However, it is certain that these men had fire, perhaps gained from natural conflagrations and carefully pre-served. We do not know whether they had begun to cook their meat, which would have made it more nutritious by releasing amino acids and sugars and also helped in its preservation, or whether they sim-ply used fire for warmth and protection against the more dangerous beasts.

By this point a thoughtful reader will be wondering, when did *homo erectus* live? The dating of prehistoric development is actu-ally a very serious problem, which will be discussed later in a spe-cial essay. Unfortunately the remains of *homo erectus* which have been found elsewhere are very few—until recently there was only one jawbone of this type from all Europe. On this very limited evi-dence *homo erectus* has usually been placed about 400,000 to 500,000 years ago—halfway from Australopithecines to the present.

Homo Neanderthalensis

After the appearance of *homo erectus* men of this type continued to live over many parts of Europe, Asia, and Africa and made their tools in much the same way for several hundred thousand years. The tools themselves survive, but in the human record itself there is a period of perhaps 200,000 years from which we have too few bones to be able to see the physical development of man.

M. M. Gerasimov, Liudi kamennogo veka, *pl. IV.*

Reconstruction of a Neanderthal youth about 16 years old, from a skull found at Le Moustier. Mikhail Gerasimov (1907-70), the son of a Russian physician, decided at the age of 10 that his life work would be to learn how to model the physical appearance of a man from his bones. In 1950 he founded a special institute, which has become famous not only for its historical reconstructions but also for its valuable work in murder cases.

Presumably this lack is merely accidental. Human bones do not usually survive well in the acid soils of hot climates and are delicate in the best of conditions unless they have become fossilized; when they are found, they often have been crushed or deformed by the pressure of an overburden of soil. Archeologists always are very excited when they do discover remains of early man, but at this point their work becomes extremely difficult. The evidence is likely to be important, but it is difficult to dig out and preserve. Moreover, one cannot treat the bones of one's great-great-grandfather in the casual way one disposes of the bones of a wild boar or deer.

At all events, the next type which appears in the record is also the first which was discovered in modern man's search for his origins. In 1856 a very unusual skull was found in the Neander valley (*Thal*) in Germany. One of the fathers of modern anatomy dismissed it as the malformed skull of an idiot, but we now know it belonged to *homo Neanderthalensis.*

Generations of this kind of man lived from about 110,000 to 35,000 B.C. At the latest count 68 sites which he inhabited have been located in Europe, North Africa, and the Near East; remains of 155 persons have appeared at these sites, almost all of which are cave-shelters. This may appear a small number, but it far surpasses the total of all earlier examples of mankind.

Neanderthal man until recently was reconstructed as bent over and shuffling as he walked, but a more careful student pointed out

Hand-ax, an all-purpose tool which Neanderthal man made in much the same way for tens of thousands of years.

University Museum, University of Pennsylvania

that the specimen which had been used for the reconstruction suffered severely from arthritis. In reality Neanderthal man stood upright, about 5′3″ high, and was heavy-boned with a barrel chest; his face had a low forehead with heavy ridges over the eyes, large nose, and not much of a chin. His brain capacity averaged 1438 cc., almost half again as much as that of *homo erectus.* This is, incidentally, as big as the modern average, but the size of his forebrain (which apparently is the seat of memory and thought) seems to have been smaller. Still, if a Neanderthal man were dressed properly, he could go into any grocery store without drawing attention.

Neanderthal Culture ❀❀❀❀❀❀❀❀❀❀❀❀❀❀❀❀❀❀❀❀❀❀❀❀
Neanderthal man, obviously, did not have a grocery store at his disposal, but he seems to have been an efficient hunter and gatherer of food; his meat at least he seems to have barbecued. Earlier forms of man had probably been largely scavengers of anything, plant or animal, which could be eaten raw, though at times they had driven animals (including even mammoths) into swamps and there butchered the helpless beasts. For weapons Neanderthal men still relied mainly on wooden spears and stones, which may have been tied together to make a *bola,* but one may speculate that their hunting groups were larger in size than those of *homo erectus* and also better organized. They were even willing to face and kill the great cave bears which lived in the vicinity of the Alps.

The stone tools at their disposal are of a variety of types for which scholars often use the label Mousterian (from the name of a French site where they were first found). Large "hand-axes" were made from the core of a flint module and were all-purpose, especially useful in butchering. Other, smaller blades were made from flakes struck off a core and could be employed, for example, as scrapers of skins or knives (from scratches of these blades on the teeth of Neanderthal man we can tell he was usually right-handed).

In Mousterian and other later styles, flint-makers displayed considerable skill and forethought in preparing a core shaped like the back of a tortoise and striking flakes from it to produce a fairly wide range of implements. These tools, however, do not seem to have been designed with an eye to working wood or piercing bone; bones were used mainly in helping to crack the flints. No Neanderthal beauty appears to have dressed herself in a shell necklace (as we

The cave-shelter of Shanidar; a view of the excavation was given on p. 7.

shall find in the next stage), and warriors did not yet string the teeth of the wild animals they had killed. We do not even have bone needles to show that Neanderthal men, who lived at times in very cold periods, could sew together the skins they probably wore.

Neanderthal Burial
By at least 50,000 B.C. Neanderthal men and women were in the habit of burying or commemorating their dead. One fascinating Neanderthal site which illustrates various aspects of burial has been dug in recent years at Shanidar, in the Kurdish hills of northern Iraq. Its excavator, Ralph S. Solecki, spent months prospecting for the right cave-shelter. Prehistoric men liked a home which faced south, for illumination and the sun's warmth, with a dry floor, near water, and close to good food supplies. The great shelter of Shani-

dar, 82 feet wide and 26 feet high at its opening, reaches back into an area of up to 175 feet broad and 45 feet high; it overlooks a valley about 15 miles long with a number of side canyons into which animals could have been driven for slaughter. Solecki excavated here on four occasions, in a region earlier called an "iron-bound untamable fastness—a regular Brigand's Paradise," until a great Kurdish revolt prevented him from further work.

At Shanidar the deposits of man and nature are up to 45 feet thick; the lowest 28 feet represent about 60,000 years of Neanderthal life—and death. The first skeleton found (Shanidar I) was of a man about 40 years old who had been killed by a rock fall. His right arm had been deformed from childhood, to judge from his shoulder blade. His lower arm may even have been amputated, for his worn front teeth had been used to help in holding objects. He had also lost the sight of his left eye and was arthritic. Yet this venerable elder, who could scarcely have hunted himself, had played his part in the Shanidar community, perhaps as fire-watcher and cook. After his unfortunate end the survivors seem to have placed rocks over his remains and held a funeral feast.

Nearby were Shanidar II and III, who were likewise killed by a rock fall. From the evidence of the ribs of Shanidar III he had at the time been recovering from a spear wound—an accidental result of the hunt, or a deliberate attack? In another Neanderthal cave-shelter (on Mount Carmel in Israel) remains of a man were discovered who clearly had been killed by a spear point; and at one site in Yugoslavia unmistakable evidence of cannibalism has been found.

To balance the picture of Neanderthal man, however, there is Shanidar IV, a male discovered with two females and a baby in a deliberate burial in a cleft among the rocks. Solecki, who had been trained as an archeologist at American sites, was in the habit of saving soil samples as he dug; seven years after the discovery of Shanidar IV a French paleobotanist in Paris got around to peering through her microscope at the samples taken next to this burial. To her amazement she discovered great quantities of flower pollen and other remains. The body of Shanidar IV had certainly been strewn with hollyhock and other kinds of the wildflowers that grow in these hills. From the types of flowers used in the burial she could deduce that the death took place in the period late May to early July. How many other Neanderthal flower burials have gone unnoticed?

Neanderthal Man

We have spent a longer time in looking at Neanderthal man than at earlier types, partly because the evidence is more extensive, partly because he seems definitely to have been "a man" in his physical structure, careful tool-making, and burial patterns. At Shanidar about 40 Kurds winter in the shelter nowadays; the excavators estimate that in Neanderthal times the group of residents was perhaps in the range of 25 people. The problems of their social organization and other non-physical aspects of life will be considered later, after we have come to the end of the food-gathering stage of human history; but the fact that Neanderthal man deliberately buried his dead is a very suggestive illustration of a human mentality.

What Is Man?

This chapter has discussed the major stages of early mankind in chronological order. It is time to consider a problem which is hidden in the discussion: Just what do we mean by the term "man"?

Can we define man in terms of the size of his brain? As we have seen, this distinction has some use in contrasting the first forms of man, but among modern men the dimensions of one's brain do not correlate very well with genius. An average European male today has a brain capacity of about 1450 cc.; idiots, however, have been known to measure up to 1700 cc. A great thinker of the Renaissance, Erasmus, had only 1255 cc.; Lenin, the Russian revolutionary leader, had a huge brain. To apply a proverbial expression, it's not what one has but what one does with it that counts.

In recent years students of prehistoric man have often defined man as a creature who manufactures tools in a constant, repeated pattern. This test has considerable usefulness but also serious limitations. Tools made of wood, bone, and similar materials do not survive well in most conditions; and there is evidence that chimpanzees, for example, can fashion useful objects for their needs. If we do take stone tools as a rough indicator, then mankind has existed certainly for 1 million years and quite probably for 2½ million years.

There are other aspects of "man" which one must not overlook. For some of us, man is distinguished from all other creatures by the possession of a soul or, in other terms, conscious intelligence. Historians as a whole feel that spiritual matters are not directly subject to historical investigation. Yet we have all known people whose vital spark has enabled them to conquer great physical or social handicaps; can we attribute all of man's change over many thousands of years to factors outside his own will?

It does appear that humanity has continuously used and changed its environment for its own needs. For hundreds of thousands of years there was perhaps more adaptation of natural surroundings than direct alteration; but over the past 50,000 years the evidence for human manipulation of nature becomes more and more apparent.

No single quality of man will serve as a mark which allows the historian to announce, "At this point man appeared." On the contrary, we must consider physical, mental, and cultural aspects in defining the nature of man. It might be more accurate to say that man has made himself over a very long period of time.

CHAPTER 2

The Later Food-Gatherers

The Appearance of Homo Sapiens. In the previous chapter we considered virtually all of human history; that is, we have reached about 35,000 B.C. At this point a new type of man appears in western Europe who seems to have supplanted a form of Neanderthal man which had become more and more inbred. The new variety of mankind is ourselves, in other words the kind called *homo sapiens* ("wise man").

At the present time there is no certain evidence as to where *homo sapiens* first appeared or, for that matter, how he came to be. Some of the Neanderthal skeletons from the Cave of the Kids on Mount Carmel appear almost to be a cross with *homo sapiens,* or perhaps might be considered a transitional type. Physical anthropologists today incline to feel that our kind of man did somehow develop, perhaps in the Near East, out of a less specialized Neanderthal type than that which has generally been discovered in Europe. But until there is further information we could equally well guess that he had come from outer space.

There is no need to describe *homo sapiens* as he appears in the finds of Cro-Magnon and other French sites, for one can look around at one's fellows and see essentially the same body-type. What does need emphasis is the fact that all living men today belong to the same species. Over billions of years the processes of evolution have produced on earth some 2 million species of insects, 20,000 species of fishes, and other varieties of life in profusion; but whatever our stature, color of skin, or way of life all of us are "wise men." Students of prehistoric man as a physical type, incidentally, cannot yet agree as to whether other kinds of man simply died out as sideshoots or whether they essentially amalgamated to produce one species.

Biological unity, however, does not mean cultural unity. From the appearance of *homo sapiens* onwards we can distinguish more and more local cultural diversities. There is, it may be added, no clear evidence as to when the so-called races of man (mainly distinguished by skin color and type of hair) came into existence or why they developed.

In most of our story we shall be considering men of white skin, for they were the inhabitants of the ancient Near East and Europe. In meeting peoples such as Indo-Europeans or Semites, Sumerians and Maglemosians, one must keep in mind always that these names do not mean human types defined physically by variations in the shapes of their skulls (long-headed or round-headed) or color of eyes. Rather, these terms describe *cultural* groups which are often distinguishable by language, and had very different ways of life.*

A Burst of Progress ❊❊❊❊❊❊❊❊❊❊❊❊❊❊❊❊❊❊❊❊❊❊
In the period from about 30,000 to 10,000 B.C. mankind made advances of a variety not seen earlier. Twenty thousand years may seem an eternity to us, but measured against the preceding hundreds of thousands of years of apparent stagnation these changes took place in a moment. Even in the Shanidar remains of Neander-

---

* To make this point clear let me note that the *only* way one can distinguish an Indo-European is when he opens his mouth and talks, whether it be English, Russian, or ancient Greek. Indo-European is simply a group of related languages. Some people who are blond and blue-eyed speak such a language, but in early times in central Asia there was an Indo-European group (called Tocharic) which may well have been yellow-skinned. Students of genetics have never discovered any way in which the language one speaks is related to one's "blood"—or to one's intellectual capabilities.

thal man, which cover a period of 60,000 years, Solecki was unable to see any real changes in the tool equipment.

Why did this progress, which led on to even more rapid advance after 10,000 B.C., take place? Or, since it is sometimes helpful to stand a difficult problem on its head, why had there been the earlier stagnation? Parenthetically, we might go on to ask if "change" should necessarily be viewed as an inevitable part of human life, or if the developments which so many of us talk about today as revolutionary are really anything more than surface alterations when we compare them to the really great changes in the past.

In looking at early man one might perhaps conclude that "we" are more capable of achievement since we have a bigger brain. Certainly it is true that the physical aspect of man which has altered the most since Australopithecine days has been the size of his brain, and this adaptation must have been a useful one for man's advancement. The brain of modern man is almost three times as large as that of an Australopithecine; on the other hand it is not noticeably bigger than that of Neanderthal man. The fact already noted that the forebrain has become more prominent in *homo sapiens* may be related to his progress, but one must be careful in assuming that modern man can "think" better simply because he has a slightly different skull.

M. M. Gerasimov, Liudi kamennogo veka, pl. XI.

Early *homo sapiens,* reconstructed by Gerasimov from a skull found at Cro-Magnon.

The Environment of Man ✿✿✿✿✿✿✿✿✿✿✿✿✿✿✿✿✿✿✿✿✿✿

Perhaps *homo sapiens* advanced because he was better able to change his way of life as his environment changed. Up to this point we have not taken into account the physical world in which prehistoric man lived, for essentially the environment was always hostile and difficult—and yet capable of giving man, even as a parasite, what he needed for survival. All animals were wild, and some were very dangerous. Prehistoric man faced creatures such as saber-toothed tigers and cave bears; down to almost the end of the food-gathering stage lions, mammoths and elephants, rhinoceroses, and hyenas were native to western Europe.

Across the hundreds of thousands of years of early man the climate of the world was subject to marked oscillations. The reasons for these variations are still not clear; the major mountain-building and essential separation of the continents had occurred before man appeared. The most evident marks of these climatic alterations are the repeated advances of glaciers in the northern hemisphere from about 3 million B.C. onwards, and rainier or drier periods in the southern hemisphere. The "pluvials" or rainy eras cannot yet be firmly related to the glaciations, though it does seem likely that temperature changes occurred in much the same fashion everywhere.

By the early 20th century geologists had determined the existence of four major glaciations in the Alps, but for Europe and North America as a whole there seem perhaps to have been three significant waves of glaciers during man's existence. Neanderthal man lived just before and into the last of these Ice Ages (about 70,000 to 8000 B.C.), during which the ice ebbed and advanced several times. At its maximum the ice was up to 2 miles thick in North America and covered one-quarter of the land surface of the globe, as far south as New York, London, Berlin, and Warsaw.

Homo sapiens appeared in western Europe just before a temporary recession of the glaciers in this last Ice Age and then survived their final advances down to about 10,000 B.C., after which they began a major retreat. Very possibly some of man's development in this period was actually a response to the environment; but in that case one still faces the question, why did not earlier man respond to *his* environmental alterations in the same way?

What is apparent in the archeological record is the real, if limited, advance marked by the culture of Neanderthal times. We may speculate that during the millennia after 110,000 B.C. mankind became more numerous and also developed greater and greater sureness in maintaining its life by hunting and gathering food. Thus from about 35,000 B.C. *homo sapiens* had an inherited base from which he could progress rapidly, and some aspects of his physical structure may have aided in this tremendous advance.

History is often compared to a river. This idea emphasizes its inevitable, slow flow in time. Yet if we look at a river like the Nile, it does indeed flow sluggishly through the swamps of the Sudan, but then breaks suddenly over great rapids or cataracts, and finally slips rapidly down the valley of Egypt to the sea. So too human development at times is slow. At other points generations engage in tremendous leaps, like the quantum jumps of atomic particles or the unexpected mutations in biological species.

The Great Hunters

The popular picture of prehistoric man is of a shaggy creature huddled over a fire in a dark cave. Actually it is not very sensible to suppose that men usually dwelt in caves which were always without sunlight; Shanidar is a much better example of the open rock shelter which men were inclined to prefer, at least in the winter. Sometimes they built a lean-to under the overhanging rock; at one French site mammoth tusks had been set upright as a fence for the shelter.

In the summer (and sometimes even in winter) men also lived in open-air settlements. Our evidence for this kind of home is naturally not as good as that for cave shelters, but archeologists have recently explored a number of open dwellings on the great central European plain reaching from Germany through south Russia. One of the most interesting of these, Dolní Věstonice, lies in southern Czechoslovakia on a natural migration route for mammoths and other prehistoric animals. Amateur enthusiasts discovered the site late in the 19th century; for a number of years before World War II it was dug (most of these finds were burned in a castle by the retreating German army); and further careful work has taken place since the war.

Dolní Věstonice was inhabited from about 27,000 to 23,000 B.C. Experts have carefully analyzed the wood, the pollen, even the

Czechoslovak Academy of Sciences, Prague

Drawing of Dolní Věstonice. On the right are skin-shelters and huts; to the left are great masses of mammoth bones.

snails found at the site and concluded that through most of the period the area had permafrost with stunted pines and firs on the surface, the type of landscape known as taiga. The average yearly temperature in the colder periods ran about freezing. Nonetheless a group of human beings ranging up to 100 in number seems to have lived here the year around; its pattern of existence was more complicated and diversified than any down to this era.

On the lower part of the site, near a swamp, men cut up their game. Farther up the slope they built tent-like huts with stones and posts supporting skins and two hearths. One large structure (9 by 15 meters) was presumably a wind-break screen. The tools comprised as great a variety as one would find in a modern household kit. Heavy, well-made stone implements served as axes and as scrapers. Sharply pointed awls could be used to pierce bone, shell, or skin. There were many narrow blades, including the long thin chisels called burins, a distinctive tool of the period after 30,000 B.C. Spears now apparently had stone points; the main value of this addition was to promote hemorrhaging in wounded animals. Tools were also made out of bone and ivory, including antler shovels, and the inhabitants could work wood well.

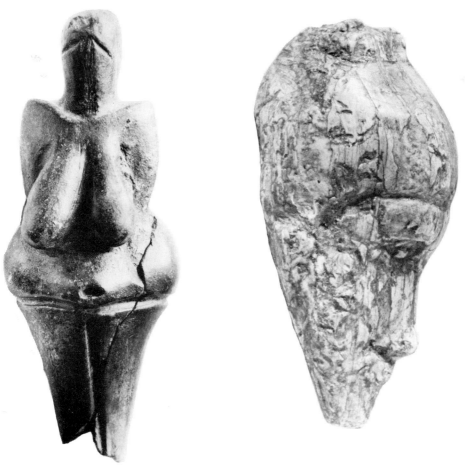

Above are the Venus figurine found at Dolní Věstonice and a side-view of
the female head discovered near the grave of the possible magician. Below
is the head of a wolf, modelled in clay and then baked.

Czechoslovak Academy of Sciences, Prague

At Dolní Věstonice, as at other sites of the period, objects appeared which suggest men had interests beyond hunting. There are bone pipes or flutes, which were certainly intended for musical purposes. Beads and perforated shells indicate decoration (at one Italian site a child had evidently worn a skirt entirely covered with sewn shells). In the ashes of the largest hearth at Dolní Věstonice was found a baked clay-and-bone female figurine, shapeless of head and legs but with heavily accentuated torso. This type of figure, called a Venus, appears at many sites of early *homo sapiens.* Some scholars argue it is an embodiment of a Mother Goddess or fertility emblem. Others dismiss this speculation as a modern concept, and suggest that men liked to make female figurines; in an age when food was not always plentiful, they might well have conceived of the ideal female as plump. In some of these stylized figurines, incidentally, the hair is suggested enough to show that women carefully frizzed it or gathered it in "buns."

Up the slope from the main settlement at Dolní Věstonice lay a hut about 6 meters round with a ring of limestone blocks supporting wooden roof posts. Inside was a hearth or oven with more than 2000 fired clay clumps, some of which were clearly models of heads, bodies, and feet of animals. Pottery was not to recur in human history for about 20,000 years; even more exciting is the problem, why were these objects made in this isolated location? It is hard to escape the feeling that a specialist whom we might call a magician worked here to produce replicas of the animals which the men of Dolní Věstonice hunted, and that he (or she) made spells over the clay figures to aid in the hunt.

There is yet another surprise at this site. Off to one side was the grave of a woman about 40 years old. The earth had been sprinkled with what appears to have been red ocher, a common custom in graves of the period; the body had been firmly covered by 2 shoulder blades of mammoths, perhaps to prevent her return to haunt the living. The corpse was provided with what seem to have been unused flints. During her lifetime the face of the woman had had an asymmetrical left side, due to paralysis of the nerves and weakness of the muscles. Not far from this site—but several years before its discovery—the excavators turned up a small sculptured human face with exactly the same physical characteristic. It is very unusual in the Venuses of this period to see any attention to the face; could this little head have been a real portrait? If so, was the woman who was so carefully buried a great magician or spell-maker of the tribe?

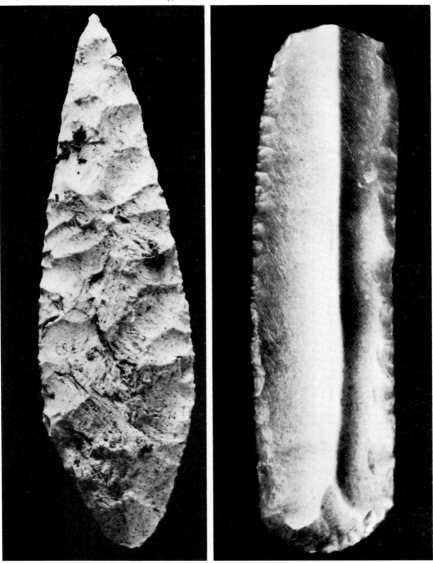

Typical stone tools of early *homo sapiens*. On the left is a laurel-leaf point; on the right, a burin.

Men in Western Europe   ✽

The area which archeologists have explored most thoroughly is western Europe. Here some other open-air homes of hunters and flint collectors have been excavated, and also a great number of inhabited rock-shelters have been located. Some of these have remains of incised or engraved figures, usually in forward areas where sunlight was available. Farther back in caves, often in very remote corners, paintings of animals or, less often, of human beings have been discovered. As art these paintings are often magnificent; their purpose is more fiercely debated (see the special essay on pp. 59-65). The occasional presence of simple stone lamps in which fat could be burned shows that by this time man was quite capable of making fire when he needed it.

The stone and bone implements of western Europe are much like those of Dolní Věstonice and show continuous patterns of evolution. The rows of stone tools laid out in display cases in modern museums may appear uninteresting at first sight, but they suggest far from dull conclusions. For one thing, there is ever greater variety and specialization of use from the simple choppers of *homo erectus* through the subsequent hand-axes and flakes to the burins and other blades of *homo sapiens*. Also, the forms of tools became ever more precise and clear of shape. Men had embarked on a road of conscious analysis which has led to the computers and accurate measuring tools used in modern laboratories.

The stages of development in the equipment of *homo sapiens* are given identifying names; the tools at Dolní Věstonice, for instance, belong to the Gravettian culture. Noticeable too are the regional variations, which become ever more marked. As man progressed, his way of life or "culture" grew more specialized; but interconnections between different areas can thereby be detected. Men in central France, thus, were buried with shells which came from the Mediterranean over 100 miles away. So too in Africa and western Asia a variety of cultures of early *homo sapiens* has been identified by the careful work of many scholars, and more will undoubtedly appear in later years. Rather than considering all these detailed aspects, however, it is time to think a while about what man had done up to about 10,000 B.C.

No one knows the exact purpose of these intricately carved rods of horn, made in the days of the cave painters. Notice, however, how complicated and precise the designs are.

Looking Back at Prehistoric Man

A famous English philosopher, Thomas Hobbes, once defined the life of early man as "solitary, poor, nasty, brutish and short." Short at least it was. On the basis of skull sutures and dental conditions a recent anatomical estimate suggests that 49% of Neanderthal men died by the age of 20, and 40% between 21 and 40; only one example seems to have lived past 50. Early *homo sapiens* did no better: 54% died by 20, and 35% between 21 and 40. If one considers just those people in both periods who lived past 20, most women were dead by 30 while most males lived past that year.

One must always approach with caution any statistics which are as narrowly based as these are—the death rate among children was probably even higher—but the general picture seems frightfully clear. Shanidar I, who survived to the age of 40 despite his missing right arm and left eye, was a very venerable elder.

Hobbes's idea that early man was solitary, on the other hand, is certainly wrong; but what truth lies in his other adjectives, "poor, nasty, brutish"? Here we run into fascinating contradictions in modern opinions.

If we look at this disagreement for a moment, it may help to explain one aspect of history which often bothers beginning students of the subject. That is to say, people feel that since history deals with facts and dates it ought to provide positive, firm answers as to why events took place and what their meaning is. Yet anyone who reads two historical studies of the same subject will probably discover that their authors present very different explanations even if they tell the same facts.

Why do scholars disagree, for instance, about the nature of the life of prehistoric man? The reason is not simply that we do not have enough information, for we would never have enough evidence to prove one view or another. On the contrary, the root of modern arguments about early man is the fact that scholars hold very different views about the nature of man today and his possibilities for the future.

One school of thought idealizes the early part of human history as a golden age, an idea which goes back to the Biblical picture of the Garden of Eden. This theory, often called the "cult of the Noble Savage," considers that civilization is corrupting. Mankind was much better before life became complicated, before there were class distinctions, before war and imperialism existed.

ALLEY OOP By V. T. Hamlin

Newspaper Enterprise Association

Alley Oop in a cave-man setting. Do the situation and the dress of the characters suggest in any ways the transfer back to prehistoric times of modern attitudes?

Another school, to which Hobbes obviously belonged, thinks that man has advanced through the ages. Scholars of this stamp emphasize the possible evidence for cannibalism in prehistoric man and the rigorous severity of his life. It is this line of speculation which basically dominates the comic-strip picture of prehistoric man as sub-human in appearance, with ax and skins, grabbing early woman by the hair and dragging her back to his cave. A great deal of pre-history, incidentally, is written from a modern masculine point of view; but obviously the female sex was at least as important in the survival of early man.

Certainly any male in his right senses would have tried to get a woman, though the hair-dragging part of the picture seems absurd. Women not only produced and reared children across their many years of dependence; they also probably tended the fires as a rule; and it is quite likely that their provision of food by plant-grubbing, berry and acorn gathering, and the capture of small animals was much more certain than the occasional successes of the male hunters. One theory of prehistoric life, particularly favored by Marxist prehistorians, is that the females were then the more important sex and that the first societies were matriarchies.

Social Conditions ✿✿✿✿✿✿✿✿✿✿✿✿✿✿✿✿✿✿✿✿✿✿

In reality we must always remember that we have only physical evidence and that any hypotheses which go beyond that evidence must always be taken as guesses. One problem, for instance, which may have concerned the reader is the pattern of early social life.

Did men and women live in families like ours or in more harum-scarum fashion?

One way to attack this problem would be to look at our modern relatives in the ape world. The results point in every direction: Asiatic gibbons pair off, single male and single female with offspring; but gorillas and other apes live in groups consisting of a senior male, several females with offspring, and perhaps some very junior males. In this "harem" pattern there are often independent groups of bachelor males.

Another method of approach would be to read the reports by anthropologists and other scholars about modern primitive societies. Very generally these peoples dwell in monogamous relations; but the rules of who can marry whom are often extremely complicated. The relations of father, mother, and children—and relatives —are very usually not those which we would consider instinctive; but they vary widely from one society to another society. However, one must always be very careful in arguing back from modern primitive peoples to the conditions of prehistoric man. So-called "primitive" groups today have had a very long time in which to set their patterns.

If we turn back to prehistoric man himself, it is reasonably clear that he did live in groups. One can also see advance in the fact that the size of the tribe at Dolní Věstonice was clearly much bigger than that at Neanderthal Shanidar; monkeys and apes do not seem capable of enlarging the size of their groups. It would perhaps be reasonable to argue from the hut patterns at Dolní Věstonice that the group there was subdivided into smaller groups, which may even have been "families." A student might expect that burial practices would throw some light on the problem we are examining, but in reality they do not. Even in historic cemeteries one would not be able as a rule to tell just from the skeletal evidence (without tombstones) what kind of family structure existed.

The figures for life-expectancy which were given earlier also suggest that in the early clumps of mankind life was always more in the threat of extinction rather than in that of a population explosion. The age of puberty in prehistory, given the problems of lack of food, was probably much higher than today. Statistics from Manchester, England, suggest that in that city the age of menstruation for girls of the lower classes was 15.7 years in 1820 but for girls of middle and upper-class backgrounds it was only 14.6 years at the same time; thanks to better diet and health conditions the age for girls of the latter type has now sunk to 12.9 years.

If women in prehistoric times were mostly dead by 30, they could not have produced many children, and of those about half would have died before the age of 20. Time and time again catastrophes of nature or illness must have wiped out a little pocket of mankind, and one can only speculate how scattered hunting groups managed to interrelate so that each genetic pool did not become highly inbred.

It is small wonder that a recent estimate suggests there were less than half a million men alive at any one time in the whole world early in the food-gathering period and only about 3 million by 10,000 B.C. The fact that mankind survived so that we could be born in the present generation is really almost a miracle. Or, put in another way, whatever sexual, family, and political organization prehistoric man created it did suffice for his survival.

Intellectual Capabilities

Another area of early life which much interests modern scholars is that of intellectual achievements, and especially its religious concepts. Here again a sober historian must be amazed by the sweeping pictures which can be drawn—and how much they disagree with each other.

From Neanderthal times on men did tend to bury their dead with some care and at times sprinkled the corpses with flowers and red ocher. Again, at least from early *homo sapiens* onwards there are what appear to be shrines, decorated with deliberate artistic products. There are also, at Dolní Věstonice and elsewhere, the famous Venus figurines.

What does the evidence mean? Whether men conceived of an after-life or simply wanted to ensure that some kind of ghost of the dead did not return we do not know, though the use of red ocher suggests to some students that the survivors tried to give the dead the life-giving character of blood. The theories about sympathetic magic or fertility cults which have been deduced from cave art will be considered in the special essay on this subject, but to sum it up here these speculations usually show more about modern ingenuity than about early man. It is, in particular, very doubtful if prehis-

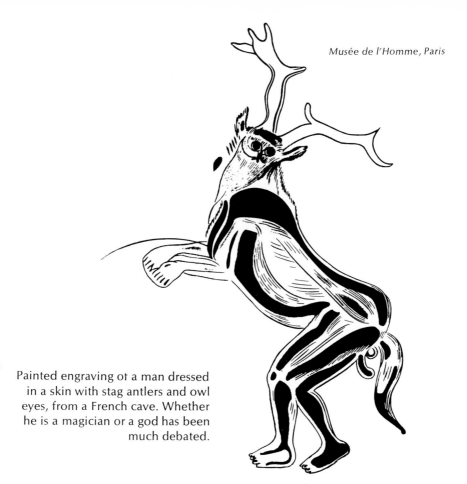

Musée de l'Homme, Paris

Painted engraving of a man dressed in a skin with stag antlers and owl eyes, from a French cave. Whether he is a magician or a god has been much debated.

toric man had any great interest in "fertility" for itself. The safest conclusion—on the basis of the actual evidence—is that early man was quite capable of some kind of "religious" belief without trying to be specific as to what this belief may have been.

More certain testimony to man's intellectual capabilities is his ability to make implements in the same pattern generation after generation. In view of the shortness of life children probably learned the skills of their elders at a very early age. As the tens of thousands of years went on, mankind changed and improved its techniques ever more rapidly; we have already noted the wide variety of tools in the period after 30,000 B.C. One scholar has estimated that from one pound of good flint men in the *homo erectus* stage could get about 8 inches of good cutting surface, Neanderthal man (with flakes) about 40 inches, *homo sapiens* from 10 to 40 feet of blades such as burins.

Speech

One interesting way to sum up the major problems in understanding prehistoric man is to ask if he talked. The physical evidence of his skulls will not answer this question, though it is clear that the physiological equipment we use for talking was intended primarily for breathing and eating. The skillful analyses of modern linguistics have been applied to the earliest languages which were written, but they do not help us penetrate very far back into purely oral stages. The answer in the end depends on our general view of prehistoric man.

That men, like other animals, could utter cries of alarm, mating, discovery of food, and so on is not at issue; the problem is when did men have means of deliberate communication? One way to reach a decision is to decide why men would need to talk. Children could be reared without real verbal activity; possibly the hunt and driving of wild animals could be carried out with only cries; the ways of making stone tools could be learned just by imitation. Some scholars feel that the fact Neanderthal man buried his dead proves he could verbalize. Others think one of the distinguishing marks of *homo sapiens* was his ability to talk. Students of this school prove the "fact" especially by arguing that the cave painters "must" have been able to talk.

There is an entirely different way of looking at this problem. One of the most distinctive physical characteristics of mankind, which he shares with very few other animals, is not often noticed: he can sit upright for long periods. And as we have all observed over the years men do like to sit. If we conjure up in our mind's eye a group of Neanderthal men or even *homo erectus* sitting around the entrance to their rock shelter, did they just sit quietly and admire the wild landscape before them? Or did they verbalize ideas stirring in their brains, and tell stories and legends? They would, after all, not have needed to know all a modern dictionary; the pidgin English spoken in some parts of Oceania has only about 60 words, but these are enough for a translation of the Bible.

To return to a much earlier remark, we often think that prehistoric man simply grabbed prehistoric woman by the hair and dragged her away; it is just as possible that he looked lovingly at her and told her how beautifully her hair was frizzed. Maybe, to carry this idea further, he even learned how to make a Venus figurine so as to give her a present.

Musée de l'Homme, Paris

In this late prehistoric drawing from Spain a man (or woman) is on a rope ladder, gathering honeycomb from a hole in a rock while the bees buzz about. Another figure below, not shown here, holds the ropes. Did they need to be able to talk to each other?

The Spread of Mankind

However little we may really know about man's intellectual and spiritual capabilities, by 10,000 B.C. he certainly had become a very skillful hunter, dangerous to every other type of animal, and already had begun to exterminate some species. By this date mankind had developed a social and physical culture which enabled it to live in any area of the globe from the edge of the northern ice masses to the fringes of the complete deserts.

This includes the Americas. At the present time scholars feel that man entered North America from Siberia at a time when he could walk across what is now the Bering Strait. The occasionally suggested idea that he came by boat—and brought with him ideas of pyramids and so on—is really disguised science-fiction. Geologists now think that there was a land-bridge to Alaska, not covered by ice, about 26,000 to 20,000 years ago and then again about 12,000 to 11,000 years ago.

Unfortunately we cannot yet tie the tools used by earliest man in America firmly to any relatives in Siberia, and so it remains uncertain which of these two periods (or perhaps even earlier) is the one to choose. The first widespread datable evidence of man's presence in the New World consists at this time of the Clovis and Folsom stone tools, somewhere before 10,000 B.C. (see the photograph on p. 70); but within the next three thousand years man had made his way to the very southern tip of South America. When the scattered skeletal remains of these early American hunters can be dated still remains subject to debate; but enthusiasts for woman's place in modern society can happily point out that the earliest in the United States seem to be those of women.

CHAPTER 3

The Food-Raisers

Introduction ❀❀❀❀❀❀❀❀❀❀❀❀❀❀❀❀❀❀❀❀❀❀❀❀❀❀
Great changes had taken place after the appearance of *homo sapiens*. As a result mankind stood on an intellectual and technical level by 10,000 B.C. which was far higher than that in any earlier period. Men were ready, at least in some areas, to take a giant step forward and began to raise their food.

In doing so they may have been encouraged by the climatic changes after 10,000 B.C. Within the next two thousand years the glaciers began that retreat which is still going on. The climate in Europe proper turned rainier, the forest grew, and the fauna moved northward. North Africa and western Asia seem to have had a climate similar to that of the present day, though somewhat damper. Climatic changes, however, had occurred frequently in earlier periods. Only now was man sufficiently advanced so that he could alter his mode of life drastically to fit the new natural surroundings.

Dead Ends ❀❀❀❀❀❀❀❀❀❀❀❀❀❀❀❀❀❀❀❀❀❀❀❀❀❀
Over most of the earth men simply continued to hunt their food, and in the rain forests of Europe hunters even found it a more complicated task to locate and kill the reduced variety of wild animals which lived in heavily wooded country. On the seacoasts, which became longer as the seas rose at the end of the ice age, men col-

lected and ate oysters with such enthusiasm at some points that they left kitchen middens or banks of oyster shells many feet thick. Maglemosian men, as the inhabitants of north-central Europe are called in the centuries after 10,000 B.C., also fished from canoes with nets and hooks, gathered nuts and fruits, and hunted with bow and arrow as well as with the spear. The bow is the first true machine we know to have been made by man.

If we can trust a limited base of statistics, men of the era tended more often to live past 20 than in earlier periods, though about half of those alive at 21 were dead by 30. Thanks to their intensive cultivation of a variety of food resources such people often became rather sedentary, so that they lived in the same site for year after year. Perhaps as a result they domesticated the dog and tended to polish their stone tools in order to work wood better with adzes, chisels, and gouges. Still, such cultures as the Maglemosian represented a dead end, from which further progress would be limited and slow. To break out of the limitations of a food-gathering economy required a real revolution, the domestication of plants and animals.

Men and Plants

Prehistoric peoples had eaten anything not poisonous which they could gather or catch. The remains of hackberries appeared in the Choukoutien deposits; later sites often show that their inhabitants ate a variety of berries, fruits, and wild cereals. The residents of one Danish community slashed the throat of an unfortunate victim as a human sacrifice and threw him in a bog; his excavators were able to analyze his stomach contents and show how mixed his last meal had been.

Deliberate cultivation of plants, however, seems to have been discovered in only three areas. In eastern Asia men turned to raising millet, yams, and rice; agriculture here may have been as early as anywhere else in the world. In the New World beans, squash, potatoes, corn, and gourds were cultivated in central America and in Peru. The most important step by far was the domestication of wheat and barley by the peoples of the Near East. This development can be tentatively placed somewhat before 7000 B.C. From this region the idea of agriculture spread outward to most of Eurasia and Africa.

Early Farmers in Mexico ❀❀❀❀❀❀❀❀❀❀❀❀❀❀❀❀❀❀❀❀❀❀

Although we shall look carefully at the Near East in a moment, the one place where scholars at the present time can see best the shift of man from wandering bands to settled villages is the valley of Tehuacan, some 125 miles southeast of Mexico City. Here R. S. MacNeish and other investigators have been carefully following the traces of the early inhabitants. After years of patient work they have constructed a fascinating picture of the steps in the change to agriculture.

Initially the occupants of the valley wandered rather erratically in search of food, but as the climate grew drier after about 9600 B.C. men found game harder to locate and settled into regular seasonal migrations. In the winter people lived off the hunt; in the summer they gathered leaves, fruits, and seeds in the better-watered parts of the valley. During the period 6700-5000 B.C. men still migrated, but in the summer cultivated squash, amaranth, and chile. During the fall they picked fruits and raised avocados (which require some irrigation). By this time the small bands in which people were ordinarily grouped occasionally consolidated during the summers into larger centers along the rivers.

After 5000 B.C. men began to raise corn and beans as well as gourds, but it is estimated that their food consisted of 52% wild plants, 34% meat, and 14% agricultural products. People still moved about; not until about 3400 B.C. did they usually live in one place, with limited movements in the winter. What we might term true villages, that is, permanent occupation of the same sites by a primarily agricultural population, do not appear until about 1500 B.C. By this time the farmers were concentrating on corn along with chile, beans, and squash and had much improved the yields of their crops so that they had reserves for winter. Other results were the making of pottery and a marked increase in population, which led on to the extended use of irrigation, the construction of temples, and other marks of civilization proper after 850 B.C.

Throughout this long development the changes in the ways of gaining food were related to major alterations in rainfall but became ever more conscious and skillful. Equally important were two non-physical developments: the evolution in territorial and settlement patterns and the enlargement of social structures. The rise of agriculture, it must be emphasized, was not a simple, easy process of just starting to grow crops. Man had to domesticate not only plants and animals but also himself.

Ancient agriculture required much hand labor. The scene from an Egyptian tomb shows plowmen with digging-sticks in the lower right corner; in the upper left, men are carrying a basket with reaped wheat. Below is an Egyptian figurine of a woman grinding grain with a stone which she rubbed on a flat surface.

Changes in the Near East after 10,000 B.C. ✿✿✿✿✿✿✿✿✿✿✿✿

Nowhere in the Near East has archeological exploration yet uncovered the consecutive stages which have been mapped in the valley of Tehuacan. In a few places patterns of movement from summer to winter homes have been traced, but in general one must piece together bits of evidence from many different sites to try to form a picture of the developments from 10,000 to 7000 B.C. There are major gaps which may be filled in the years to come.

Even the climate of the area is subject to great debate, for some scholars still seek to explain the origins of agriculture simply in terms of a human reaction to assumed increases and decreases in rainfall. It does appear that before 10,000 B.C. conditions had been sufficiently colder and drier that the upland hills such as those about Shanidar were not inhabited; but by 8000 B.C. the climate of the Near East had settled into very much the modern pattern. The lowlands proper were mostly hot and dry. During the winter adequate rain (over 20 inches a year) fell in the mountains and lower hills of modern Turkey, Syria, Israel, Iraq, and Iran to support two kinds of wild wheat (einkorn and emmer), six-rowed and two-rowed barley, and various root vegetables. In these hilly areas the wild ancestors of sheep, goat, and pig also lived, and in later times it was to prove useful for man that copper and other metals turned up in the hills both as ores and as native lumps.

At various places men had developed their food-gathering skills sufficiently so that they could live fairly continuously in the same site. A good example is furnished by the inhabitants of the rock shelters on Mount Carmel and nearby open settlements, who are called Natufians. They adorned the terraces in front of their rock

Straight sickle of antler with flint teeth, used by the Natufians of Mount Carmel to harvest wild grain.

British Museum (Natural History)

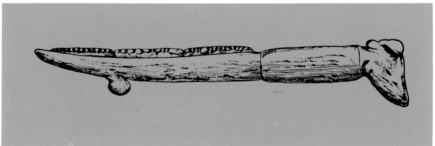

shelters with low stone structures, the purpose of which has not yet been discovered, and they rebuilt their rock huts several times on the same spot as old homes fell to pieces. The Natufians also employed a fairly extensive equipment of tools, largely of the types found at Dolní Věstonice and elsewhere, and buried their dead carefully with beads and headdresses.

These people must have had an assured food supply. In large part they were hunters and fishers with the usual equipment of this period—harpoons, fishhooks, spears, bows, and so on. What is most intriguing is the suggestion that they were almost on the verge of discovering agriculture. The Natufians certainly reaped the wild grasses of the neighborhood with straight bone sickles set with small flint teeth, and they processed the kernels with milling and pounding stones. Huts at times had built-in storage places and fireplaces.

Neither here, however, nor at some interesting sites in the hills of Iraq can one *prove* that deliberate agriculture had begun. Probably the development was as halting as that which appears in the valley of Tehuacan. In a settled community just below the cave of Shanidar the remains of what appear to have been domesticated sheep have been discovered in levels of about 9000 B.C.; but carbonized grains of wheat and barley have not yet been found in Near Eastern sites before about 7000 B.C.

Early Villages

The problems involved in the appearance of agriculture did not begin to exercise scholars seriously until about the time of World War II. Thereafter one of the most devoted explorers of the subject has been Robert Braidwood, who excavated the little village of Jarmo on the slopes of the Zagros mountains in 1950.

A few years earlier a field inspector for the Iraq Directorate of Antiquities had happened to be in a nearby village and asked its headman if he knew of any antiquities. The headman replied that the villagers had never heard of any, offered his visitor a cigarette, and drew out a prehistoric flint to strike a light. The inspector found out where the flint had been discovered and made a surface collection of flints and other objects, which were duly lodged in the museum at Bagdad. When Braidwood appeared in search of a likely site, Jarmo was recommended to him.

The results proved remarkable. The mound itself covered about

3 or 4 acres and seems as a rule to have had some 20 to 25 houses, or about 150 people. In the top 5 of the 16 settlement layers pottery was found, going back to about 6100 B.C. Below that lay levels created by earlier farmers to about 7000 B.C. The wheats and barley were very close to the wild forms; men also ate among other crops lentils and field peas and gathered pistachio nuts and acorns. The goat and perhaps the dog were domesticated, and also perhaps the pig, but sheep and cattle were still hunted. The farmers built rectangular houses of irregular slabs of mud, which were plastered.

Beside stone tools for woodworking and grinding grain they also had the habit (which is very common in early farming villages) of making figurines of females and animals. Whereas the Venuses of early *homo sapiens* must remain a riddle, there can be little doubt that farmers did have religious and magical ideas concerning the

Among the many discoveries at early Jericho were human skulls, the faces of which had been restored in plaster with inset cowrie shells for eyes. Reverence toward one's ancestors, marked by the careful preservation of their skulls, appears in many primitive societies.

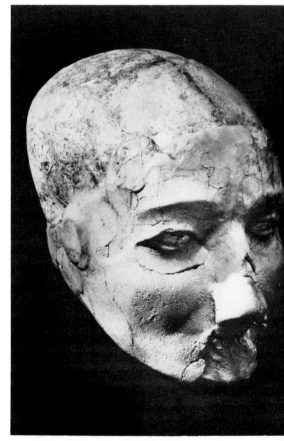

British School of Archaeology, Jerusalem

fertility of their crops and flocks, on which their lives depended more and more; for later, in early civilized societies, a Mother Goddess was an important religious concept.

Even more impressive than Jarmo are two other sites which have been subsequently excavated. Jericho in the Jordan valley was an oasis, fed by a perennial spring, which hunters inhabited by 8000 B.C. In the years just after 7000 as many as two thousand farmers who lived there encircled their settlement with a great stone wall, one tower of which stood 40 feet high with a 7-foot ditch cut out of solid limestone before it.

The farming village at Çatal Hüyük in south-central Turkey was even larger, covering 32 acres with 50 feet of deposits. Here houses stood close-packed, each entered by a hole in the flat roof. The platforms along the edges of the rooms served as beds, a small corner for the male by himself, a larger one for the female and perhaps the children. This specific fact we know because the dead of Çatal Hüyük were exposed on platforms in the open air until they were reduced to bones, and then the remains were carefully buried under the appropriate bed.

In addition to the usual figurines the residents of Çatal Hüyük adorned their plastered walls with paintings of "goddesses" (sometimes shown giving birth), animals, and birds (perhaps vultures). Men here had domesticated sheep and goats as well as probably the dog; they raised 3 kinds of wheat (emmer, einkorn, and spelt) together with barley, peas, and lentils; and they gathered apples, almonds, hackberries, acorns, and pistachio nuts. A large part of their food, however, was still procured by hunting.

The Physical Results

All over the Near East there remain mounds of farming villages yet to be explored, but it is time to consider the tremendous results of this advance. In truth it is perhaps the most decisive step man has ever taken.

The material consequences are evident in the mounds themselves. Men lived at the same site generation after generation, near springs and good farming areas, and piled up debris at an unprecedented rate. Houses made of mud-brick walls and reed or thatch roofs will last a considerable period if they are kept plastered, but eventually a great storm or outside attack brings destruction. Then the inhab-

itants pull down the remains and build on a higher level. Buried in the debris are stone tools of all kinds; excavators have found copper beads or other trinkets made of native copper by 6000 B.C.; and occasionally there are the imprints of woven cloth or, at Çatal Hüyük, the painted representations of what look very much like Oriental rugs of today. Spinning whorls and loom weights also attest the growing use of wool. Flax was grown both for its seeds, rich in oil, and as a source for linen; but skins still continued to be worn.

By 6100 B.C. rude pottery was being made at Jarmo, and other evidence suggests that its origins should be placed at least several centuries earlier. Very soon potters began to decorate their wares by incisions or by painting, so that modern archeologists can detect regular patterns of pottery evolution and the movement of artistic ideas from one area to another. Some of these aspects are considered later in a special essay (see p. 66).

The practical utility of pottery also deserves mention. In itself the manufacture of baked vessels out of clay called for a certain amount of skill and helped to produce specialists. In the pots agricultural surpluses could be stored and also cooked. Men could now boil food more easily than by using a leather container with hot pebbles.

In the earliest periods of gathering wild cereals and then raising

J. Mellaart, Çatal Hüyük, pl. 71

Drawing of a fresco at Çatal Hüyük, showing stags, and male dancers with weapons and tambourines. This may have been a hunting dance.

them, men sometimes parched the wheat and barley, ground it, and made a gruel. At other times it was malted (allowed to germinate), and this process at times led to the interesting result of fermentation and thus of beer. The human digestive tract probably had to face very considerable alterations with the introduction of farming.

The Social Results

If the winter rains failed, a village might get no crops. Some settlements seem to have tried farming and then given up the effort because of local problems in adapting crops. Still, the fact that men also continued to hunt, fish, and gather wild nuts, berries, and other objects may have been a sufficient safeguard to ensure against real disaster. On the whole agricultural life became far more secure and orderly. The social results of this way of life were at least as important for mankind as the increased variety and quantity of physical objects it made possible.

How the first farmers of the Near East came to tame either plants or animals remains a matter of guesses. We might suspect that food-gathering peoples had occasionally stored their surplus grain and that they came to speculate on the fact that some reserves sprouted.

A herd crossing a river (from an Egyptian tomb relief). One herdsman carries a calf which looks back at its mother, who lifts her head anxiously. In general, the raising of plants and of animals went hand in hand; nomads who lived off their flocks were a late development.

Since women probably did most of the grain-collecting, any statue of the First Farmer should probably be cast in female form; but the rise of agriculture certainly did nothing to help raise the position of women. On the contrary, in the civilized societies which followed upon the early villages masculine dominance seems firmly established as an ancestral pattern.

Another result was a considerable increase in the population. Settlements of the size of Jericho and Catal Hüyük had never existed before. In part this increase was the result of what seems clearly to have been a somewhat better chance that children would survive to maturity; partly it was the consequence of increased food supplies. Early farming, however, was a very primitive culture with digging-sticks and hoes; animal power was not hitched to a plow until the

4th millennium B.C. Yields were probably not more than 4 or 5 grains of wheat or barley for every grain which was planted. The evidence of the Tehuacan valley may warn us not to exaggerate the rate of population growth; in the Near East the great expansion of population occurred after men had moved down into the fertile river valleys.

Farming settlements were much more consciously organized and interconnected. From the situation at the beginning of historical times one may infer that authority lay with the elders of each village, who applied tribal tradition to the conduct of daily life. Individual independence of action must still have been a virtually unknown concept, and men worked together within a close-knit society. One of the earliest villages in Egypt even had communal granaries (pits in the ground lined with coiled basketry).

Each early farming village was virtually self-sufficient. Nevertheless its inhabitants were linked to the physical and spiritual world which lay about them. The fact that the citizens of Jericho felt compelled to devote very extensive labor toward walling themselves is significant. More peaceful connections with outside tribes were attested by the presence of foreign objects and materials, such as the discovery of obsidian and cowrie shells at Jericho. By 4000 B.C. the spread of ideas in the example of pottery designs can be traced over hundreds and hundreds of miles in the Near East and even farther.

The Spread of Agriculture

Once the domestication of plants and animals had begun, men seem to have needed time to become accustomed to their great achievement in the Near East, as they did in the Tehuacan valley. The farming villages changed very slowly over the millennia from 7000 down to and past 4000 B.C. One feels that mankind was in another of its "static" periods.

The concept of agriculture, however, was easily transmitted and was rapidly seized by other peoples. In part the spread of agriculture from its home in the Near East may have reflected the expansion of its own population, based on the greater food resources, but more often other food-gathering peoples probably picked up the idea via the thin lines of prehistoric trade.

Historians cannot fully determine the dates or routes of agricultural expansion, unless the styles of pottery or the use of figurines give clues. Eastward, farming turns up in northern China along the

Yellow river by the 3d millennium. The early styles of Chinese pottery have at times been linked with those of the Near East and south Russia; but true proof of any connection remains to be found. Greece and the southern Balkans had farming villages almost as soon as in the Near East, by the 7th millennium. Northern and central Europe was held back by the widespread forests and the presence of a much different, continental climate.

Whereas the earlier inhabitants of western Europe seem at times to have been more advanced, as in cave painting, the population of the area north of the Alps remained in a backwater from after 10,000 B.C. until the time of Christ. In and after the 6th millennium peasant cultivators made their way up the Danube in a technique of slash-and-burn, moving on when the roughly cleared land was exhausted for farming purposes. Probably agriculture also spread westward by sea to other districts of Europe; there were farmers in Britain by 3500 B.C. South of the Sahara agriculture did not become common until the 1st millennium B.C.

Mankind in 4000 B.C.

The period from before 1,000,000 to 4000 B.C. is almost unimaginably long. Its story too must be long, even if one omits many of the variations in ways of life which existed in Eurasia. Unfortunately there is not a single hero or heroine in the tale; for we do not know the names of any prehistoric persons.

Rather, the hero must be mankind as a whole. The physical alterations of our ancestors, from Australopithecines through *homo erectus*, Neanderthal man, and *homo sapiens*, seem to have been a relatively minor increase in size of body and a considerable enlargement of the brain. Apart from the Neanderthal footprint illustrated on p. 6 we have no direct evidence on the outward appearance of early man, and so we do not know if they were hairier than we are or had different skin colors.

The great developments which can be seen are alterations in the way men lived. These changes at first were immeasurably slow, then more rapid. True, mankind has not generally lived just as we do at this moment, and prehistoric men did not think about themselves, about other men, or about the world in our framework of ideas. This fact suggests one of the great values of history. We may be the children of our fathers and mothers—and we may be more affected by that inheritance than we sometimes admit—but we do not think entirely as our parents do, and we may think very differently 20 years from now. Man is a creature of infinite possibilities. Very rarely can one say with any justice, "This is the only proper way to think or act."

As the story has been told, it may leave the reader feeling that mankind has followed a straight, inevitable line of progress. This conclusion would not be true, for men pursued many paths and sometimes wound up, like Maglemosian man, in a virtual dead end.

Somewhere else another group would take a different course, and eventually their more backward neighbors would learn from the example; the men who had once lived in the Maglemosian hunting culture finally became farmers. Although there was no one road which all men had to follow, interconnections between groups across Europe, Asia, and Africa did exist. At least by the age of farming a major idea of technique which was developed at one spot made its way with remarkable speed over thousands of miles.

A deeper problem needs just to be mentioned here: was it a matter of mere chance that humanity developed as it did? If we do not call it chance, then what did move history? This is a problem which concerns each of us, for consciously or unconsciously we must have some view as to why our own lives go as they do; but to problems of this type every person must give his own answer.

As measured against the whole course of man's existence, by 4000 B.C. virtually all of it was over. Down through the 18th century all "advanced" societies still remained agriculturally based. That is to say, in the England of Elizabeth I or the America of George Washington probably 90% of the population made its living by farming. Yet even if 4000 B.C. seems only a brief moment ago there were other significant changes yet to take place. In particular, the farmers of the Near East had developed their agricultural techniques, their social structure, and their numbers so that they were ready to leap once more, this time to the level of civilization.

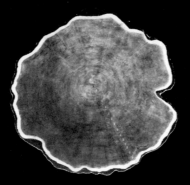

Dating the Past

Cave Art

The Uses of Pottery

DATING THE PAST

Students of history probably grumble about "learning dates" more often than about any other aspect of the subject. And yet when we get to a period for which there are no written records we very soon begin to ask, Just when did this or that take place? If a story lacks dates, it becomes vague. We cannot correctly relate events in one area to those in another; and worst of all it is impossible to judge the speed with which changes have taken place.

For as long as scholars have explored the prehistoric period, they have sought to establish valid methods of dating what they found. Down into the 19th century the early history of man was divided by the Flood which Noah and his family survived. The thunder-stones and other obviously primitive materials were thus called antediluvian, "before the Flood." When a stone hand-axe turned up at a London site in the 17th century together with the tooth of an elephant (of a type which we now know was extinct in historical times), the conclusion was that a Briton of the 1st century after Christ had fought a Roman elephant there.

After geologists had established a fairly firm sequence of major eras in the earth's history, this sequence provided a framework which is still very useful. The last of these geologic eras is called the Cenozoic which is usually subdivided into the Pleistocene epoch, or glacial age, and recent epochs (since about 10,000 to 8000 B.C.). The Olduvai gorge furnishes a beautiful cross-section of most of the Pleistocene age; but even if a single skull is found in an isolated context, it can often be given an approximate date by the sedimentary stone or gravels in which it has appeared.

Archeologists also find helpful the remains of the flora, especially the pollen, and also the bones of animals associated with a discovery of stone tools or human skeletons. In Europe, for example, there were three major successive species of elephant: *meridionalis* in the earliest part of the Pleistocene, *antiquus* in the middle part, and the mammoth in the days of late Neanderthal man and early *homo sapiens*. Also useful are the remains of hyenas, rhinoceroses, and other animals.

All of these methods of dating have been ever more carefully refined in recent years. The study of cores drilled in the floors of the Caribbean and other ocean bodies has helped to define the temperature fluctuations of the Pleistocene epoch. Again, fluorine analysis of bones is very valuable in estimating their relative ages.

Historians would like, however, to have absolute dates B.C., and other techniques have been developed for this purpose. Almost one hundred years ago a Swedish scholar noticed that series of layers of earth were deposited by melting glaciers. These layers are called *varves*, from a Swedish word meaning "periodic repetition," and occur in regular pairs, a coarser sediment and then a finer clay for each year. By careful measurement scholars have been able to count back varve deposits to before 10,000 B.C. There is another method of counting annual "deposits" in the form of tree rings. In the American Southwest this method has been developed so that a well-preserved cross-section of a California tree can very often be given an absolute date back 6000 years before Christ.

One of the most notable recent techniques was announced in 1949 by Willard Libby, who received a Nobel prize for his discovery. The method entails measurement in organic deposits of carbon-14, that small part of carbon which is radioactive. When living matter ceases to grow, it stops adding C^{14} to replace that which has been disintegrating. Since this radioactive form of carbon has a half-life of 5730 years (plus or minus 40 years), analysts can find the decrease of this element in an organic substance such as charcoal and can thereby locate the approximate age of this material. Theoretically C^{14} dating can be extended back to about 70,000 B.C., but before 50,000 B.C. the residue is usually too small to be properly measurable.

Extensive determination of C^{14} dates has pretty firmly established the chronological pattern of early *homo sapiens* and later Neanderthal man so that we can relate chronologically a site like Shanidar in Iraq with another in Czechoslovakia such as Dolní Věstonice. Naturally, the historian cannot trust any one C^{14} date, for the material tested may have been contaminated or otherwise give an erroneous date (statistically a C^{14} date has 2 chances in 3 of being approximately accurate). Furthermore, comparison of material dated historically in Egypt or by other methods with C^{14} tests suggests that the production of C^{14} did not necessarily take place at an even rate across early times.

More recently it has been discovered that potassium 40 disintegrates at a regular rate into calcium 40 and argon 40. Since radioactive potassium has a half-life of 1.3 billion years, this method can be used especially for eras before 500,000 B.C., such as the earlier levels at Olduvai gorge and other Australopithecine remains. When one adds tests based on nuclear-fission tracks and paleomagnetism, it is clear that scientists have created a considerable arsenal of dating skills.

Archeology, it may be noted, is a very special subject, which will not be discussed by itself in this book; the historian seeks to interpret the results of the archeologist's work. Still, our investigation of prehistoric man must have demonstrated how many specialists are needed by an archeological expedition: paleobotanists for the plants, paleontologists for the bones, geologists for the natural environment, soil experts, and many others. Only by their cooperation do discoveries like Shanidar and Dolní Věstonice become truly useful.

CAVE ART

Very soon after his appearance in western Europe *homo sapiens* began to decorate rock shelters and caves. Earlier, he had apparently painted his own body and engaged in tattooing; then he turned to improving his environment artistically. During the period from 28,000 to 10,000 B.C. over 112 sites in France and Spain received more or less elaborate attention. For so long a span of time this is not a great number, but the decoration is amazing. The painted bulls in the cave at Altamira were discovered in 1879, but it took until the end of the century before all scholars accepted the fact that this art was very early.

From the rock shelters we have mainly incised or engraved figures, sometimes in low relief; for real painting was not likely to survive in an open atmosphere. Elsewhere one can wind along limestone cave tunnels, occasionally crawling on hands and knees or again mounting a chimney into yet another passage; and finally there will come a hidden cavern or recess with painting after painting. In a few places clay sculptures have been found.

Usually the subjects are animals. Out of 2188 examples which one scholar counted, over half were horses and bison; next followed mammoths, ibexes, and wild oxen. But there were also woolly rhinoceros, reindeer, even one rabbit, and a few fish and birds. Human beings occur sometimes; there are also "signs," which have been taken to be traps, huts, or symbols of male and female. If one finds a group of animals, they do not ordinarily seem arranged in a composition. In fact

The French caves which have cave paintings lie in limestone terrain like that shown above.

they can be drawn on top of other animals, shown in different sizes, or placed sideways and upside down at the pleasure of the artist.

The paints were made from natural earth pigments and are various shades of ocher, red and brown being more common than yellow. Black (oxide of manganese) was also used, but not blue or green. At times some sort of brush or stick was the tool of the painter. He could also employ his fingers (hands are often drawn or outlined, sometimes with fingers missing), and perhaps the artist used a tube to blow paint.

Although the paintings reflect living creatures, the terms "naturalistic" and "realistic" are not altogether correct descriptions of their style. From cave to cave the manner of drawing will differ markedly. In part the differences are the product of development over the centuries, but there is less change in this respect than one might imagine. In the examples that modern art historians would call the best the cave artists

60   ON THE TRACK OF EARLY MAN

showed amazing ability to represent animals with an economy of line. Artistically these vigorous representations were not to be matched until historic times; the paintings at Çatal Hüyük, for example, are far more stiffly stylized and conventional than those of the caves.

The great problem in cave art is to determine why it happened. The artists must have liked to draw animals, but they would not have gone, fire and paints in hand, far into hidden recesses just to make pictures.

Cave art also included reliefs. This female from Laussel holds a bison horn and was originally painted with red ocher.

Jean Vertut

Jean Vertut

Incised figure of a bison from La Grèze. Notice how the artist has used only a few lines to create the impression of a powerful animal.

Generally scholars believe that they were serving their hunting communities by performing acts of sympathetic magic. That is, drawing or modeling animals would help to produce real animals and would ensure success in the hunt, particularly if one engaged in voodoo-type chants and actions. In one cave there were found clay animals which apparently had been struck by spears.

In this particular example, true, the hunters had to be almost on their hands and knees, perhaps using daggers, and there are other logical difficulties in explaining all cave art as sympathetic magic. For one thing, the animals shown do not correspond very well to the animals the bones of which turn up in the French and Spanish sites. Other scholars accordingly suggest that painting of animals could accompany the initiation of the young into the adult tribe, for footprints of children do appear in some caves. The possibility of really religious inspiration, as against pure magic, has also been argued. Recently there have been ingenious but not very convincing efforts to explain all cave art as reflecting the male/female principle. In one of these theories horses and deer stand for the male, and bison and mammoth for the female. On the whole it seems likely that a variety of motives could have impelled the men of the period to paint or sculpt.

We may not be able to put ourselves inside the minds of these artists, but their products still survive to show abundantly that they did have minds. Insofar as their motives were magical or religious, one may conclude that specialized consultants of the spiritual world were beginning to appear in hunting tribes; but the painting itself is evidence enough that specialized skills had emerged. Whatever its roots, cave art is one of the greatest testimonies to the wide range of abilities and interests of early *homo sapiens*.

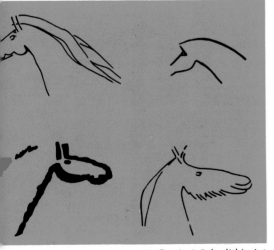

These sketches of the heads of horses may suggest how varied were the styles of cave artists.

P. Graziosi, Paleolithic Art

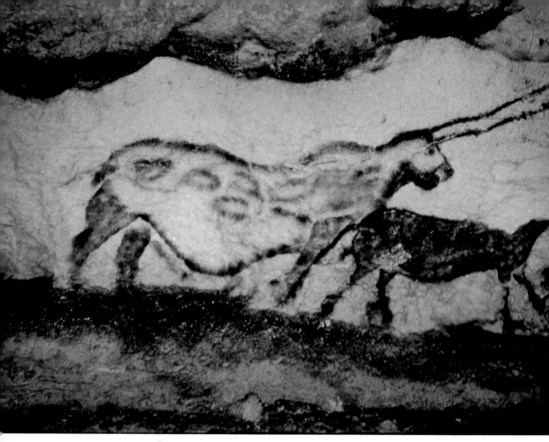

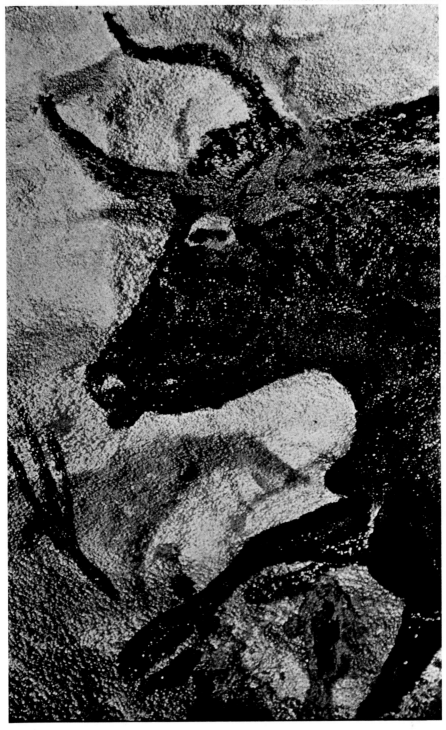

One of the greatest series of cave paintings was found at Lascaux. Above left is an imaginary animal called a "unicorn"; below left is a horse; above is a bull.

THE USES OF POTTERY

As long as men changed their homes often or even in a winter-summer sequence it is not likely that they would have been interested in making pottery—cumbersome to carry far and all too likely to break. Even after men had settled down in villages which became agricultural, they often concentrated on making stone vessels or baskets which might be lined with clay. At some point in the period from 7000 to 6000 B.C., however, men in the Zagros foothills of Iraq and Iran (and possibly elsewhere) discovered that baked clay containers had a variety of uses.

The early potter built up his vessel out of spiral coils of clay or successive strips, scraped the sides smooth, and often burnished the surface with a pebble or other tool. To keep the clay from cracking he added grit or straw. After the pot had been slowly dried, it was baked either in an open fire or in a kiln. If the air is excluded from the kiln and the gas of the burning substance is rich in carbon monoxide, the pot usually turns black. If air does enter, then a red color results. Over the centuries the potters became more and more skillful in refining their clays and in firing their products.

Some modern African tribes delegate the task of pottery-making to the women. We do not know which sex was responsible in the early villages, though some archeologists argue the shape of thumbprints indicates they were made by females. Certainly by historic times potters were generally male specialists. By this time they used the potter's wheel on which they could "throw" their vessels with greater speed and dexterity; this device was known in Mesopotamia before 3000 B.C.

For ancient men, down through the fall of the Roman Empire, pottery had many uses. Large pots were storage vessels for oil, grain, and other products and could be employed as coffins. Smaller vessels were used in cooking, eating, and drinking, though a modern man will wonder how well they could be washed or otherwise cleaned of bacteria. When a Greek poet advised his fellow villagers to take a new pot straightaway to the local magician to pass a charm on it, he may unconsciously have had hygenic problems in mind.

Very soon after men learned how to make pottery, they also began to decorate it. Sometimes the potters used a shell or comb to make linear, incised patterns; at other times they "painted" the surface with a fine slip of clay. If the resulting vase were fired skillfully, the design often took on a different color from that of the body of the vessel (thus the term red-on-black which is used for vases of this type). Some of the most magnificent painted pottery in the early Near East was produced in the 4th millennium B.C. at Susa. By historic times the well-to-do in the Mesopotamian cities were able to afford tableware and

An Egyptian potter, forming a vase on his "wheel," a clay disk which he rotated with one hand while he shaped the pot with his other hand.

Oriental Institute, University of Chicago

The main subject of the decoration of this vase from Susa (4th millennium B.C.) is a goat whose horns sweep around in a great curve. Above is a row of hunting dogs; around the rim are birds with long necks, as if they were trying to drink the contents of the goblet. This vase is considered one of the greatest pieces of pottery from the early Near East.

Another painted vase of the 4th millennium B.C., which was found in the mound of Sialk (south of modern Tehran). The animal is a stag with stylized horns.

decorative vessels made of gold and silver, and ordinary pots thereafter were made with much less artistic attention.

For the modern archeologist pottery also has many uses. Clay pots were made in great abundance; they broke easily and were discarded; but the broken pieces survived by the thousands so that one can pick up sherds by the handful on any ancient site. A quick survey, indeed, of the top and eroded sides of an ancient mound will often help the archeologist decide whether it should be dug. Furthermore, pottery does not usually travel far from its site of manufacture. When the excavator does proceed to dig, he will find that the layers of inhabitation can be determined by the pottery as well as by the crumbled house remains. Everywhere the styles of decorating vases, and their shapes also, changed from generation to generation, whether one is investigating a site in Peru or in Turkey.

Within any one cultural area men tended to make and decorate their pots in a somewhat uniform style, though with local variations; and the historian can trace cultural movements by the spread of a style into new areas. Sometimes archeologists are too inclined to assume that the sudden appearance of a new pottery style means the migration of a people, as against the possibility of simple cultural diffusion. Still, the discovery of a new pottery style on top of a burned layer, together with changed patterns of burial, very often attests an invasion and general upheaval in an area. For all these reasons pottery is often called "the alphabet of archeology."

In 1925 a black cowhand in New Mexico, on the track of a lost cow, saw bones on the opposite side of a stream bed and investigated them. Perhaps flints had been discovered with peculiar bones many times before, but his report spurred an archeological investigation (which secured this photograph of a Folsom spearpoint lying between the ribs of *bison antiquus*). Since this type of animal became extinct about 10,000 years ago, scholarly views about the antiquity of man in North America were revolutionized.

If the flint had just been given to a museum, it would have had little scientific value. Only when a trained archeologist makes such a discovery in its original surroundings does it have its full value.

PART II

The Origins of Civilization

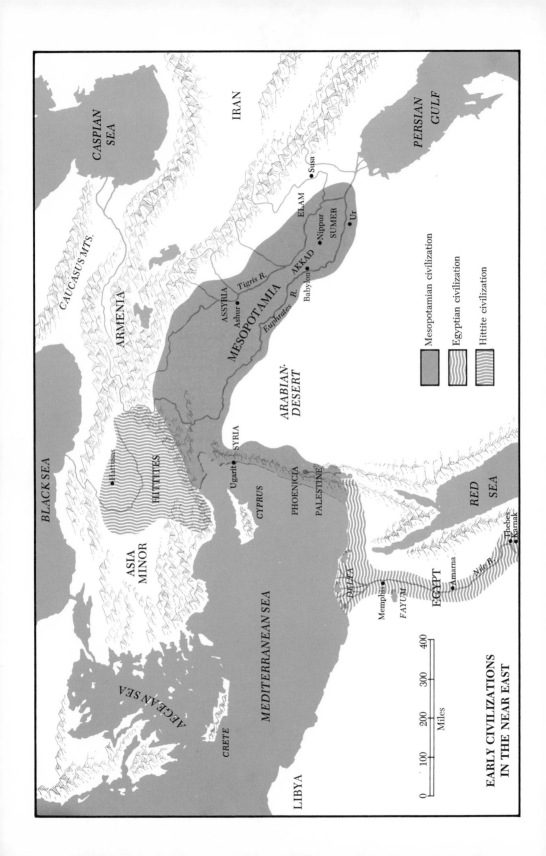

EARLY CIVILIZATIONS
IN THE NEAR EAST

Mesopotamian civilization
Egyptian civilization
Hittite civilization

CASPIAN SEA

IRAN

PERSIAN GULF

Susa

ELAM

Nippur
SUMER
Ur

AKKAD

Babylon

Euphrates R.

ASSYRIA
Ashur

Tigris R.

MESOPOTAMIA

CAUCASUS MTS.

ARMENIA

BLACK SEA

HITTITES

Hattusas

ASIA MINOR

ARABIAN DESERT

SYRIA
Ugarit

CYPRUS

PHOENICIA
PALESTINE

RED SEA

MEDITERRANEAN SEA

AEGEAN SEA

CRETE

DELTA

Memphis
FAYUM

EGYPT

Amarna

Nile R.

Thebes
Karnak

LIBYA

0   100   200   300   400
Miles

From the cave shelter of Shanidar it is 300 miles south to Babylon. If a Neanderthal man of Shanidar had been miraculously transported to the great city of good king Hammurapi (1792-1750 B.C.), he would have been astounded by its ant-heaps of brick buildings and its masses of men. The wall around one Mesopotamian city stretched almost 6 miles, with over 900 towers; Babylon numbered its male citizens in the tens of thousands. On the other hand, if we ourselves went back to ancient Babylon, we probably would find its dust, noise, and summer heat almost unbearable.

Some of the greatest changes in human social organization which have ever occurred took place when men began to live in the cities of Mesopotamia. After mankind had developed the practice of agriculture, one might assume that the step upward to a civilized level would be simple and automatic. Actually, however, many peoples of the world remained in the purely food-raising stage down to modern times; most areas that became civilized did so in imitation of districts already more advanced. Only in two areas of the earth does it seem certain that men independently created civilization.

One of these was Central America—Peru, where the Mayans and Peruvians developed civilization in the 1st millennium before Christ. The other was the river valleys of Mesopotamia and Egypt in the Near East. Here civilized societies had emerged by 3000 B.C.

This Part will examine especially the nature of civilization in Babylon about 1750 B.C.; occasionally it will be necessary to look back at the progress of Mesopotamia during earlier centuries. The many other civilized societies in the Near East of the 2d millennium B.C. cannot be considered here in the detail they deserve, for the story would then become very complicated. But we cannot entirely pass over the development of Egypt, partly because it is fascinating in itself, partly because civilization in the valley of the Nile river furnishes an interesting comparison to that of Mesopotamia.

In the foreground lies the rich Delta of Egypt, narrowing to the right or south. Beyond are the Suez canal, the Sinai peninsula, and the barren reaches of upper Arabia. View taken from Gemini IV spacecraft in 1965.

4

Civilization in Babylon

Civilization ❀❀❀❀❀❀❀❀❀❀❀❀❀❀❀❀❀❀❀❀❀❀❀❀❀❀❀❀❀❀❀❀
The idea of civilization needs precise description if we are to know
how a "civilization" differs from a "culture" of uncivilized peoples.
Among the major characteristics of civilization we may list the following: the presence of firmly organized states which have definite
boundaries and systematic political institutions; the distinction of
social classes; the economic specialization of men as traders, farmers,
or artisans, each dependent on his fellows; and the conscious development of the arts and intellectual attitudes. In the last point are
included the rise of monumental architecture (as against simple
huts), sculpture which carefully represents men, the use of writing
to keep accounts or to commemorate deeds, and also the elaboration
of religious views about the nature of the gods, their relations to
men, and the origin of the world.

"Civilization" comes from a Latin word meaning the character of
an inhabitant of a city. Usually civilized people have concentrated
their strength in cities like Babylon, but in early Egypt men dwelt
in an almost continuous series of villages along the Nile. Nor have
all civilized societies made use of writing, for in Peru records were
kept by means of knotted strings. Everywhere, however, civilization
has required the presence of some economic surplus beyond the
basic needs of its members. This surplus has been used for the artis-

tic, social and political developments noted in the preceding paragraph.

The student of man must consider civilization a great advance in history, but that does not mean everyone would praise all of its consequences. Individually each of us must pay a price, psychologically or physically, for our achievements. Mankind as a whole also paid its price for the emergence of civilization.

Class distinctions resulted in a situation where some men directed and exploited other men, whether they were free or slave. Wars and imperialism appeared, with the objectives of gaining glory for the gods of one's city or of one's king, and also for securing raw materials and booty. Psychologically the inhabitants of ancient Mesopotamia felt many stresses. At the end of our survey, even so, most of us may conclude that the benefits of civilization outweighed its disadvantages.

Mesopotamia

The area called Mesopotamia, which comes from Greek words meaning "between the rivers," lies between the Tigris to the east and the Euphrates to the west. Both rivers rise in the Armenian highlands and flow southeast to the Persian gulf. In their upper reaches, where the rivers lie far apart, the country is hilly and rolling. This region is watered by a number of major tributaries of the great streams as well as by winter rains, especially in the hills where early farmers raised their crops.

The southern part, from the point where the rivers come close together and then diverge, was the home of the first civilization. Here rain falls rarely but in sudden storms. For water men must depend mainly on the rivers, under the protection of Ea, the god of wisdom and waters. Throughout the day the great god Shamash (the sun) beats down fiercely. Violent winds unleashed by Adad, the weather god, at times lash the dull brown countryside with dust; the greatest god of the earth was Enlil, "Lord Wind." At night the ancient Babylonians could often see the stars with remarkable clarity and watched the passage of Sin (the moon) or Ishtar (the planet Venus) across the sky.

In its natural state lower Mesopotamia is a wild waste of dried mud flats, stagnant pools, and reed swamps. Apart from clay there are no building materials nor any sources of metals. This district offered little to men save its soil, which in most areas was easily worked, and a constant source of water in the great rivers. The early farming settlers had to draw off water from the high bed of the Euphrates river to irrigate their fields and then drain away this water lest the salts which it brought ruin the land even for barley. The floods of the rivers, which came irregularly in the late spring as crops were maturing, were useless and had to be warded off by further extensive labors of diking and walling. Once farmers had learned how to exploit the potential fertility of the land, nonetheless, they could expand their numbers greatly and could also produce a surplus to support non-farmers who created the complex structure of civilization.

Another significant geographical aspect of Mesopotamia is its openness. To the south and west are the vast expanses of the Arabian desert, in which lived a semi-nomadic population of Semitic-speaking peoples. From prehistoric times on these peoples entered Mesopotamia, and by the time of Hammurapi they had become the ruling element. To the east and north were the mountains of Iran and Armenia; the leaders in the first stage of civilization, the Sumerians, seem to have come from somewhere in this direction. Traders could make their way down the Persian gulf to the Indus river

Remains of the ziggurat at Nippur. Once this area lay on the banks of the Euphrates river; now it is bleak desert.

© Rapho Guillumette Pictures. Gerster.

From the beginning of civilization in Mesopatamia artists followed many different styles, unlike Egypt. The marble head above from Uruk, almost life-size, is very naturalistic, especially about the mouth. Originally the eyes and eyebrows were inlaid, and the hair was covered with a sheet of copper or gold. The alabaster head from Tell Brak (in upper Mesopotamia) is conceived much more abstractly. Both heads are essentially masks to be attached to statues made of another material, perhaps wood.

in India. Up the rivers they sought wood, metals, stone, and other resources. Mesopotamian civilization was far more receptive of external influences and spread its achievements more widely over the Near East than did the secluded population of early Egypt.

Emergence of Civilization ❀❀❀❀❀❀❀❀❀❀❀❀❀❀❀❀❀❀

Farming villages seem to have begun the difficult task of domesticating lower Mesopotamia by 4000 B.C. In the regions close to the Persian gulf it was easiest to make use of the water without extensive irrigation works, and here a number of settlements developed rapidly. While the creation of a food-raising economy had been a slow process, the appearance of civilization took place almost in an explosion, once the mass of population had reached a critical point in size and internal organization. Cities appeared in Mesopotamia during a few centuries just before 3000 B.C.

Each city, with its surrounding fields, constituted an independent country, which was no bigger than a modern American county. Within the city the priests appear at first to have been the directing elements, but there are hints that all free males formed an assembly which made final judgments. As civilization developed after 3000 B.C., however, the cities often fell into war, and their military leaders or kings became more and more powerful.

During the 3d millennium B.C. civilization moved up the rivers from its earliest home, the land of Sumer, into the river plains of the land of Akkad, as farmers improved their techniques of irrigation. The Semitic-speaking Akkadians eventually became dominant in Mesopotamia and tended to unite its little political units in a larger state. By the time of Hammurapi his own city of Babylon ruled most of Mesopotamia, and Mesopotamian civilization had become fully developed.

The Physical Framework of Life ❀❀❀❀❀❀❀❀❀❀❀❀❀❀❀❀

If one could have flown over Mesopotamia in the 18th century B.C., one would have been able to see at a glance that men had greatly rearranged nature for their own ends. The rivers still set the stage, but their precious gift of water was tapped and managed by canals which led across the farmlands to smaller channels. Each year of Hammurapi's reign was given a distinctive name by which the year was dated; his 33d was called (in abbreviated form), "He dug the canal called 'Hammurapi-spells-abundance' for the people; thus he provided Nippur, Eridu, Ur, Larsa, Uruk and Isin with a permanent and plentiful water supply."

By canals and by roads the countryside was divided into relatively regular plots which were defined by geometrical means. Farmers used wooden plows, seed-drills, and stone hoes to reap 40-fold returns of barley. Shepherds with dogs watched flocks of sheep and goats. Other areas were gardens with mud-brick walls, set about with fruit trees and overshadowed by date palms. Asses on the paths and boats on the canals carried the rich products of the fields to the vital hubs, the cities.

Every city was girdled by a moat and a wall of sun-dried brick; some of Hammurapi's year-names celebrate the restoration of this or that city's wall, or in the case of conquered countries the destruction of their protective ramparts. At the city gates the elders and traders congregated; within the sentry posts at the gates, streets wide enough for chariots and wagons ran between great masses of small, flat-roofed huts.

In these homes lived farmers who trudged out to their fields every day (though some lived in subsidiary mud-brick villages); but beside the farmers dwelt smiths, potters, and a host of specialized craftsmen. Their daily food was essentially barley, which was baked in flat sheets of bread or drunk as beer. Onions, lentils, beans, peas, dates, and various fruits were also eaten, but meat was much less common than fish.

We do not know what Hammurapi's palace looked like, but archeological evidence from contemporary kingdoms in Syria suggests that kings had guarded, extensive abodes decorated with sculpture and painting and equipped with tables, chairs, and valuable gold and silver vessels. The gods, however, were equally as important in protecting society; the great divine patron of Babylon was Marduk, whose temple was called Esagil. Beside it was a stepped mound or *ziggurat*, the original Tower of Babel of the Bible. This imitation mountain served as a symbolic focus of the powers of the earth.

Writing

By this time we have definitely passed from the prehistoric to the historic age, for men could set down their ideas and describe events in writing. The Sumerians had begun to draw conventionalized *pictograms* (representations of physical objects) on clay tablets by

Clay tablet from Kish about 3500 B.C., on which the symbols are still pictograms. Just below the head in the upper right corner is a threshing sledge (which oxen drew around and around on a threshing floor). Contrast the writing in the next picture, almost 2000 years later.

about 3500 B.C. Three hundred years later, about 3200 B.C., tablets show that the scribes of Sumer took a tremendous step by developing *ideograms* (marks expressing concepts such as "day") and *phonograms* (symbols expressing syllabic phonetic values, as we might draw a bee for the sound "be"). These ideograms and phonograms became ever more conventionalized marks, which were impressed on the clay by a pointed stick or stylus; in the 3d millennium B.C. the signs were rotated 90° for easier writing and then lost almost all relation to any original pictorial value. From the Latin word *cuneus* for wedge the Mesopotamian script is described as "cuneiform."

Most people in Babylon spoke a Semitic language which is now called Old Babylonian; but the busy scribes also preserved the epics, laws, and other materials which had earlier been written in Sumerian. The Sumerian language, which cannot be connected to any known group of tongues, eventually became a sacred, literary language, like Latin in early modern Europe. Later on, cuneiform script was used for Old Persian, an Indo-European language, and there is no reason why it could not be employed to set down English. In that case few of us would learn how to read and write, for the script involved about 500 to 600 signs, many of which are complicated. In the ancient Near East only professional scribes commonly wrote, and the evidence they provide is usually most revealing for the upper classes—unless commoners got into a lawsuit.

King Hammurapi the Just ✸✸✸✸✸✸✸✸✸✸✸✸✸✸✸✸✸✸✸

The human being who appears most often is the king of Babylon. In Mesopotamian tradition kingship "was lowered from heaven by the gods" as a guarantee of earthly order, and Hammurapi was one of the most successful rulers in the 3000 years of independent Mesopotamian history.

The year-lists of his long reign of 43 years show his unceasing concern for the walls, canals, temples, and divine statues of the land. His 22d year was known as "the statue of Hammurapi as king granting justice." Even more significant was the name of his 2d year, "He established justice in the country," which probably refers to the custom that a new king granted pardon and remission of unpaid taxes.

Hirmer Fotoarchiv, Munich

Stele more than 7 feet high on which the code of Hammurapi was engraved. The king stands respectfully before the seated Shamash, god of justice, who dictates the law to his earthly representative.

Original pictograph	Pictograph in position of later cuneiform	Early Babylonian	Assyrian	Original or derived meaning
				Fish
				Ox
				Sun / Day
				Orchard
				To stand / To go

Most famous of all is his lengthy code of laws, which was carved on a great diorite slab. This stone, which was carted off by later Elamite conquerors to Susa, was excavated in 1901. The some 200 sections of this document divide men into three classes: the upper class, the commoners, and the slaves. Punishments for crimes were distinguished by class; to give one example,

> If a noble has broken another noble's bone, they shall break his bone. If he has destroyed the eye of a commoner or has broken the bone of a commoner, he shall pay one mina of silver. If he has destroyed the eye of a noble's slave or broken the bone of a noble's slave, he shall pay one-half his value.

Women, though still relatively independent, were viewed essentially as pieces of property, especially in regard to marriage rights. Still, masculine arrogance had not yet reached the level of some later laws of the 12th century B.C., which ordered that "when she deserves it, a man may pull out the hair of his wife, mutilate or twist her ears, with no liability attaching to him." Many of Hammurapi's laws related directly to economic life and regulated contracts, irrigation procedures, debts (set at 33⅓% interests for loans in grain, 20% in silver), maximum wages, and the like.

Some of Hammurapi's legal provisions can be traced back to

earlier Sumerian codes, for class division had produced exploitation by the 3d millennium B.C. Out of the murky distance of 4000 years ago there rise outcries against oppression and injustice which sound like those of yesterday and of today; the result was the first great effort to bring justice through law and thus to protect the rights of man. In the epilogue to his collection of legal precedents and rules Hammurapi boasted:

> I rooted out the enemy above and below;
> I made an end to war:
> I promoted the welfare of the land;
> I made the peoples rest in friendly habitations;
> I did not let them have anyone to terrorize them . . .
> I have governed them in peace;
> I have sheltered them in my strength.

Hammurapi the Conqueror

Kings, however, are famous in history not solely because they care for the widow and orphan; very often their glory comes also from military valor and victories over neighboring peoples. This aspect too goes far back in Mesopotamian history; though its inhabitants shared an essentially common way of life, they often fell into conflict. Historical records show over 5 or 6 generations a debate about a small piece of territory on the frontier of 2 little states on the same branch of the Euphrates. There was a cynical proverb in Mesopotamian wisdom, "You went and plundered enemy territory, the enemy came and plundered your territory."

The first great imperialist in world history had lived 600 years before Hammurapi. This was Sargon of Agade (about 2371-2316 B.C.). According to legend, which may well be true, Sargon was born of humble parentage and served as a gardener and then royal cupbearer before usurping power. His name, which means "True King," was probably adopted after he reached the throne. Eventually Sargon conquered all Mesopotamia and extended his power even farther. A later, exaggerated account of his deeds asserts that

> he spread his terror-inspiring glamor over all the countries. He crossed the Sea in the East and he, himself, conquered the country of the West . . . He marched against the country of Kazalla and turned Kazalla into ruin-hills and heaps of rubble. He even destroyed there every possible perching place for a bird.

An early Sumerian army. The infantry phalanx with helmets, spears, and leather shields marches across the bodies of the fallen enemy.

After the reign of his equally powerful grandson Naram-Sin, however, Agade was destroyed by mountaineers from the east; and today we do not even know exactly where the city was.

Other conquerors followed Sargon on down to the days of Hammurapi, who was himself very successful as an imperialist. Upstream from Babylon there lay many independent kingdoms, including Assyria (of which we shall hear more in the next Part); but by diplomacy and war Hammurapi eventually conquered them all. The details need not be sketched; what is perhaps most interesting is that a great mass of letters survives to show how carefully he supervised his governors. One official failed to clean out a canal; on the news Hammurapi ordered him to have it done in 3 days and to report back. To another governor he had sent some archers to settle as farmers, but after 8 months they had not received their land. Hammurapi's letter gives detailed instructions and ends, "If these men are not quickly satisfied, you will not be pardoned."

Abroad as at home the political and social problems of a civilized society had come to be extensive and difficult. Hammurapi labored hard and conscientiously to keep his government efficient and his people happy. A cynic might conclude that injustice can never be eliminated in a civilized world, for Hammurapi's efforts did not end evil for all time. On the other hand, the men he ruled did expand the intellectual and artistic achievements of earlier Mesopotamian civilization as a base for the later history of the Near East.

Mesopotamian Civilization

The advances which had already taken place by the time of Hammurapi were remarkable. When men grouped their forces to create civilization, the results in every field of life were tremendous, especially when one remembers how Mesopotamia lacked natural resources and how brutal was its climate. A modern scholar has written a whole book discussing the "firsts" which the Sumerians achieved. Such a list covers almost all the major aspects of civilization.

Art and architecture are considered separately in a special essay at the end of this Part. The arts were connected especially with religion and with the kings, but it is worth noting that every man of wealth needed at least one artistic product, a seal. In late prehistoric times seals had been made in stamp form; thereafter they were carved as cylinders decorated with human and divine figures. These cylinders could be rolled across tablets to serve as legal "signatures" or across clay lumps attached to storage vessels as signs of private property.

The busy craftsmen in Mesopotamian cities inherited many of their skills in working wood, clay, or metals from earlier ages. Lumps of native copper could be found in the hills of the Near East and had been hammered into tools or decorations since the days of Çatal Hüyük (7th millennium B.C.). Copper miners had then learned how to extract the metal from ores by the 5th millennium, though they would never have been able to use the low-grade deposits which are treated nowadays.

Copper tools had the advantage that they could be precisely cast and easily repaired. Copper was softer than stone, however, so smiths sought ways of hardening it. For a time they added arsenic to copper to form bronze, but the death rate from arsenic fumes eventually led the smiths to settle on tin as the additive to make bronze. In many fields of practical technology the Mesopotamians reached a level which was not markedly surpassed throughout all ancient history. Indeed it is only in relatively modern times that men's ways of making things have significantly changed.

It was now necessary to count and write down numbers. Mesopotamian arithmetic was based sometimes on units of 10, with special signs for 10 and 100, sometimes on units of 60. In the decimal system the Mesopotamians slowly developed an idea of place-value, that is, the meaning of a sign like 1 depends on where it stands (1, 10, or 100). In much later times the Indians and Arabs took over this idea and passed it on to us. Units of 60 were especially used in

Giraudon

Naram-Sin strides victoriously up a mountain, his foot on two fallen enemies. He wears a horned helmet like a god and carries bow, battle-ax, and javelin. The stars above represent gods who give him the victory. For the first time in civilized art an effort has been made to show a landscape.

Mesopotamian Life

Figurines and plaques provide detailed information on the crafts and sports of Mesopotamia. The carpenter above is shaping a piece of wood; below are kilted boxers. This latter scene may have a religious character, for boxing was often conducted at festivities for the gods.

This weight of 1 mina was made in the reign of Nebuchadrezzar (6th century B.C.), but the writing states that it is on the scale of the weights of king Shulgi, who lived 1500 years earlier.

astronomy, where men charted the main constellations still marked on modern sky-charts; the first precise observations of the rise and setting of the planet Ishtar (Venus) were made in the 17th century B.C. The Mesopotamian year was solar but was defined in 12 lunar months, with a supplementary or intercalary month inserted about every 3 years.

Civilization also required the measurement and weighing of quantities of grain and metals. The chief weight, a talent (about 60 pounds) which was subdivided into 60 minas, remained the standard quantity down through the Greek era. Geometry began in the measurement of fields and the requirements of monumental building. The Mesopotamians could prove the Pythagorean theorem in a practical way, but never generalized their geometry into abstract theorems; this development had to wait for the Greeks.

The combination of practical skill and a lack of ability to generalize marks Mesopotamian civilization in many aspects. Still, one must not make the mistake of underestimating the tremendous strides of these first civilized thinkers merely because their approach was so different from our own.

Mesopotamian Literature

The Sumerians had been extremely fertile in literary compositions, which were copied and recopied in the schools in the days of Hammurapi; they were also translated into Old Babylonian and served as a base for ever more extensive literary works. Much of this literature consisted of proverbs, collections of dreams with explanation of their meaning, and other practical material; but some of it discussed the origins of the world and the deeds of the gods.

If we read these early myths from a scientific point of view, the tales of the gods are neither sensible nor logical. The view of life which is expressed in their repetitious verse is a primitive one in which actions are simple in cause and often brutal and passions are elemental. In explaining the nature of the universe men translated into divine terms their own earthly concepts of personal clashes and procreation. Yet these tales were so satisfying that people all over the Near East accepted them. As retold in the Book of Genesis they continued to answer men's curiosity about the Creation down to the last century.

The Epic of Gilgamesh

The greatest tale was the story of the hero Gilgamesh, two-thirds god in origin (however that could be!). This story had Sumerian roots but was more fully developed into a continuous epic about 2000 B.C. Then it spread far and wide; copies of fragments have been found in Asia Minor and in Palestine. One artistic symbol drawn from it, that of Gilgamesh strangling a lion, was handed down age after age until it appeared on medieval cathedrals in western Europe.

British Museum
A cylinder seal, when rolled across a clay tablet, produced a picture like this. The hero may be Gilgamesh, victorious over a lion.

Unlike the other myths, which were largely theological creations associated with certain rituals, the epic of Gilgamesh was centered on human figures. Essentially it was a mighty reflection on the nature of man, who strives and creates but in the end must die. Gilgamesh himself was an early historic king of Uruk; in the epic he built the great wall of the city but treated his subjects so harshly that the gods created a wild man, Enkidu, to subdue him.

Gilgamesh, wily as well as harsh, did not meet Enkidu head-on, but sent out a harlot, who by her arts tamed Enkidu—this taming is in a way taken as an illustration of the civilizing of man. "Become like a man," Enkidu put on clothing and went forth to protect the cattle against lions and wolves. The bulk of the epic then recounted the heroic adventures of Gilgamesh and Enkidu in conquering various inhuman monsters:

> Who, my friends, [says Gilgamesh] is superior to death?
> Only the gods live forever under the sun.
> As for mankind, numbered are their days;
> Whatever they achieve is but the wind!

So, while they lived, let them at least make a name for themselves.

During the course of these exploits Enkidu offended the gods (especially Ishtar), and died after a long death-bed scene of complaint against the decrees of the gods. Gilgamesh first lamented, then set out to seek the plant of eternal life so that he might bring his friend back to life. Eventually Gilgamesh made his way to Ut-napishtim, the original Noah, who told him the story of the Flood and advised him how to get the miraculous plant under the sea. Although Gilgamesh succeeded in his quest, on his return journey he lost the plant to a snake. The dead, in sum, cannot be brought back to life.

The early Greeks created a story, the *Iliad*, telling of another great hero, the half-divine Achilles, who fought in the war at Troy and there lost his friend Patroclus. If one compares the tales of Gilgamesh and Achilles, it is clear that the story of the Mesopotamian epic is balder and has less artistic unity. It is more naïve in human depiction and is far earthier (especially in the harlot scenes). Monsters are prominent in the plot of Gilgamesh's adventures, and the appeal is more to emotion and passion than to reason as is that of the *Iliad*. Yet poetically the epic of Gilgamesh was a magnificent creation; psychologically it reflects a truly civilized meditation on the qualities of mankind.

Mesopotamian Religion ※

In the story of Gilgamesh the gods determine what happens to man, even though human beings dare to oppose the gods. Everywhere in Mesopotamian civilization religion was all-important. Only because these men believed in divine support could they have had the confidence to group themselves and establish firm footholds in the difficult terrain of the river valleys. The greatest buildings, the temples, were a mighty testimonial to a human ideal. The priests who clustered about these temples were so important in early Sumerian days that the states then might almost be called theocracies or god-ruled.

Each state had its own particular patron deity, such as Marduk for Babylon; but there was a regular pantheon or group of gods for Mesopotamia as a whole. Highest was Anu, the divine force which could be visualized in the bowl of Heaven; his name meant "sky" or "shining." Then came Enlil, the active force of nature, who at times manifested himself in the raging storms of the plains. The goddess of earth was worshiped as Nin-Khursag and under other names. Last of the four creator gods came Ea, the god of waters who fertilized the ground and by extension became the patron of the skills of wisdom. To these were added 50 "great gods," who met in the assembly of the gods, the Annunaki. A host of other deities, demons, and the like also floated in the Mesopotamian spiritual world to explain the many ills and events which befell its human residents.

Anu eventually was supplanted by Marduk, who in later times could be called the Bel (Hebrew *baal*) or "lord." Ishtar, the goddess of human fertility and also powerful in war, on the other hand rose to be universally revered. In western Semitic lands she was called Astarte, and in Greece she eventually appeared as Aphrodite (the Roman Venus).

Religious festivals occurred throughout the year, as occasions to thank the gods and also to give mortal men times for relaxation. The greatest festival, called the Akitu, took place at the opening of the new year (placed in our modern March); this New Year's festival was an 11-day period of revelry, processions, and drinking. Later than the days of Hammurapi the priests recited during the festival a great myth of the Creation, called from its opening words, *enuma elish*:

> When on high the heaven had not been named,
> Firm ground below had not been called by name . . .
> No reed hut had been matted, no marsh land had appeared.

The goddess Lilith, who brings death by night, on a Babylonian plaque. She has wings, talon feet, and the crown of a divine figure. In her hands she holds measuring ropes, which may indicate the limited length of a man's life. Originally Lilith was painted red with red and black wings.

Some of the decoration of the great Sacred Way for the main procession of this festival, as it existed in the 6th century B.C., can be
seen on p. 177.

The Place of Man ❀❀❀❀❀❀❀❀❀❀❀❀❀❀❀❀❀❀❀❀❀❀❀❀❀❀

The gods, though human in appearance, paid little attention to mankind as they drank and made merry, and also abused each other in
their divine assemblies. Men feared and honored the gods; each
little state of early times was but the earthly domain of certain divine
forces, for whose ease men toiled through their lives. Once dead,
men and women could expect only to go to a shadowy, gray land
of departed spirits.

Such views suited a land that had recently raised itself to the level
of civilization by hard labor, where the climate was severe, where
the dangers of flood and sudden disease were ever present, inex-
plicable, and incurable by human means. Mankind could never
quite forget that *it* was the agent that built and tilled, and Mesopotamians had a nagging fear that they might be upsetting an order
laid down by the gods. One myth described the gods, angered by
the masses and noises of mankind, sending down one catastrophe
after another, including the Flood (see pp. 135).

In the earliest civilization social life was no more perfect than it
is today. The laws, dream literature, and proverbs show that sons
did not always obey or revere their parents, or husbands and wives
always get along—though one Sumerian proverb tells of a happy
man with 8 sons whose wife wished for more. Men had nervous
breakdowns and other evidences of strain.

Slavery and the Lower Classes ❀❀❀❀❀❀❀❀❀❀❀❀❀❀❀❀❀

Economic problems also appeared. If men fell into debt, they might
have to sell their children into slavery. "The strong man makes his
living by the work of his arms, but the weak man by selling his children." The reduction of human beings to the legal level of pure
property or chattels always has a distorting influence upon social re-
lationships, morals, and general views of human nature. A Sumerian
law, to give only one example, ordered that "If a man's slavewoman,
comparing herself to her mistress, speaks insolently to her, her mouth
shall be scoured with 1 quart of salt."

On the other hand the existence of slavery reflects the unfortunate but inevitable fact that the leisure of the upper classes and the great monuments of early times rested upon forced labor by the multitude. In other words, civilization was not lightly bought and did not directly benefit all men alike. Most of the labor force in Mesopotamia as in other slave-holding societies of the ancient world consisted of technically free men. Slaves were rarely used in agriculture, which was the main occupation of early mankind; rather, slaves lived in cities, where they were domestic servants, concubines, and artisans. As valuable pieces of capital, slaves were usually accorded a minimum standard of human needs, and at times were able to rise again into freedom through hard work.

More significant, socially and politically, than the appearance of slavery was the depression of the farmers into the position of peasants, from whom the machinery of state and religion extorted a large part of their product. Whether they lived in village or city, the peasants bought, sold, and borrowed in markets that were dominated by others. Patterns of civilization tended to split into upper and lower levels. The unlettered lower classes remained more conservative and sank into distrust of the "city ways" of their betters; the upper classes came to assume a cultural superiority.

The Values of Civilization

The preceding pages have suggested some of the problems which may be called the less pleasant results of civilization. Especially in the field of religion we can detect how troubled the first civilized men were; the imaginary monsters which appear frequently on the cylinder seals also suggest that their owners lived in a fearful world.

If one is to judge fully the meaning of "civilization" in human development, its black aspects such as war, slavery, and human insecurity need to be kept in mind. But there are at least two other elements which cannot be overlooked in a fair verdict. In the first place, can we be sure that life in a simple village was always perfect? And secondly, one must remember that civilized man attained a new economic and even spiritual level. After all the divine world of early Mesopotamia was an orderly structure, within which men could operate in a rational fashion. The gods could be appeased by their human servants through the creation of divine ceremonies and the building of temples. These men also knew, if unconsciously, how much they were achieving, and the epic of Gilgamesh is a great celebration of the daring and cunning of mankind. King Hammurapı battled injustice at home and extended his rule abroad, and could justly celebrate his achievements.

Expansion of Civilization ✸✸✸✸✸✸✸✸✸✸✸✸✸✸✸✸✸✸✸✸✸✸✸
By the days of Hammurapi the merchants who sold Mesopotamian manufactured products in exchange for metals, slaves, and raw materials no longer worked solely on behalf of the temples or even for the kings, but were largely independent agents. They traded with their fellows in guilds far and wide, down the Persian gulf, eastward into Elam, and northwest into Syria and Asia Minor. During a period shortly before Hammurapi there survive very extensive records of Mesopotamian merchants who made their way by caravan routes into eastern Asia Minor and traded from settled posts or markets in that region, under the protection of the local kings. Their letters and contracts attest how methodical and literate the patterns of business of these merchants were, even though they were 500 miles away from home.

To say that merchants, each with his cylinder seal and cuneiform tablets, were the main agents by which Mesopotamian civilization was spread across the Near East would be an overstatement; but certainly they had some part in this important development. In judging the merits and defects of civilization a modern student must not forget that the new ways were very attractive to those ancient peoples who were sufficiently advanced to be able to accept them.

In India, thus, the inhabitants of the Indus river valley and many other parts of western India were stimulated by Mesopotamian impulses to develop their own civilization in the 3d millennium B.C. The origins of Chinese civilization in the Yellow river valley are still far from clear, but chronologically this important pattern of life seems certainly to have developed after the Sumerian outburst, and a connection is sometimes argued.

More certainly the people called the Hittites created a civilized state in Asia Minor in the 2d millennium B.C. on the Mesopotamian model and used cuneiform script to write their Indo-European languages. Finally, there is a direct tie between the appearance of civilization in Egypt and its origins in Mesopotamia, as we shall see in the next chapter.

CHAPTER 5

Civilization in Egypt

Introduction ✦✦✦✦✦✦✦✦✦✦✦✦✦✦✦✦✦✦✦✦✦✦✦✦✦✦✦✦✦✦✦

Most of us know far more about ancient Egypt than we do about the Babylon of Hammurapi. Mummies are to be seen in almost any museum, and Egyptian sculpture in stone or wood is fairly common. The great pyramids and their neighbor the sphinx almost seem to have been made to have their pictures taken. When the first historian, Herodotus, sailed down from his simple homeland of Greece to Egypt, he was deeply impressed with what he saw, and observed: "I shall extend my remarks to a great length, because there is no country that possesses so many wonders, nor any that has such a number of works which defy description."

Here, however, we shall look at Egypt more briefly than we did at Mesopotamia, partly because Egypt may already be more familiar, partly because Mesopotamian influences in the history of the Near East were far more significant. Yet historically it is useful to see how the Egyptians developed their civilization from a very similar base of food-raising villages.

The civilizations of early Mesopotamia and early Egypt were alike in many respects; but there were also marked differences in political organization, religious views, and artistic spirit. Some of these differences may be attributed to minor variations in geography and climate; but others cannot be so simply explained. There is no *one* way in which civilized peoples must live.

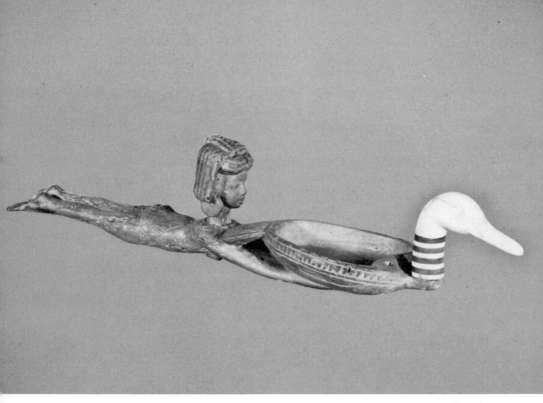

Wooden unguent-spoon in the form of a girl who is swimming and reaching out her hands to a duck. In this simple object one can feel the grace and joy in life of Egyptian civilization as contrasted to the sober, even grim, character of Mesopotamian thought (compare the plaque on p. 93).

The Nile Valley ❁❁❁❁❁❁❁❁❁❁❁❁❁❁❁❁❁❁❁❁❁❁❁❁❁

To Herodotus Egypt was "the gift of the Nile." This river rises in the lakes of equatorial Africa and the highlands of Ethiopia and flows generally northward down a great earth-fault. Seven hundred and fifty miles from the Mediterranean it breaks over the last of 6 rocky ledges or cataracts. From that point the muddy, yellow stream slips without interruption through a narrow valley about 600 miles to the Delta, where it branches out and empties eventually into the sea by several mouths. The annual floods are more regular than those of the Tigris and Euphrates rivers and are far more useful inasmuch as they cover the land in the valley during the late summer and fall, just before the time when farmers plant their seeds. A heavy popu-

The blade of this Egyptian sacrificial knife (4th millennium B.C.) is an example of the most careful flint-working ever achieved by prehistoric men. The ivory handle shows warriors and, on the lower levels, boats which are like those used on the Tigris river. This similarity is one of the pieces of evidence for contact between early Egypt and Mesopotamia.

lation could be supported once men had learned to extend the watered areas by short canals and basins. Rain falls only in the Delta, but even here is insignificant.

The Nile furnishes not only water but also a fine artery of communication which encouraged an early and lasting political unification. Egypt is relatively isolated by the cataracts to the south and the Mediterranean to the north. On either side are deserts, which come down red and bleak to the very edge of the irrigated land. When one flies over Egypt, its cultivated strip (only 4 to 13 miles wide south of the Delta) looks like a belt of green. Ancient Egyptians tended to dwell all along the river in mud-brick villages rather than in cities of the Mesopotamian type.

Stages of Egyptian History ❀❀❀❀❀❀❀❀❀❀❀❀❀❀❀❀❀❀❀❀

The population of Egypt spoke a language basically related to the Hamitic linguistic group of north Africa, but from earliest times it was much affected by Semitic influences. In the 5th millennium B.C. farming villages appeared along the edge of the upper Nile valley and on the shores of the Fayum lake (just west of the Nile). During the next millennium the farmers developed their techniques and social organization enough to master the papyrus-reed swamps and fierce animals such as the crocodile and hippopotamus of the valley proper.

Then came the same onrush which occurred in Mesopotamia as the population swelled and its skills in working stone and metal were improved. At one point direct Mesopotamian influence seems visible in the presence of cylinder seals, building in brick, and ships shaped like those on the Tigris. The Egyptians may even have gained the idea of writing from the east, but the actual symbols they used were certainly of native origin. The Egyptian script is called hieroglyphic from Greek words meaning "sacred writing," and always remained more pictorial than did cuneiform writing. Nonetheless the scribes who wrote on papyrus or carved stately rows of symbols on temples and tombs eventually came close to developing an alphabet, in which a sign stood for a single consonant. Beside this semi-alphabetic system, however, they continued to employ ideograms and syllabic signs (see the examples on pp. 103, 129).

By about 3100 B.C. Egypt became a unified kingdom. The long centuries of Egyptian history which followed are conventionally divided into the Protodynastic stage, to 2700 B.C.; the Old Kingdom, 2700-2160; the Middle Kingdom, 2134-1786; and the New Kingdom, 1575-1087. These latter dates, incidentally, can be given precisely because scholars can link an Egyptian observation of the rising of the star Sirius just before sunrise (after a period when the star was invisible) pretty certainly to the year 1872 B.C. From this point we can calculate back and forth along the long list of pharaohs or kings to settle their dates. It may also be noted that there are gaps before and after the Middle Kingdom, during which Egyptian political unity temporarily broke down. Then the local districts, called nomes, were often independent.

The first major architectural work in stone in Egypt was a pyramid in stepped form made about 2600 B.C. for king Zoser by the architect Imhotep (who himself became a god in later Egypt). The great pyramids of Gizeh, a few miles north of this example, are shown on p. 127.

Federico Borromeo/Scala

Kingship in Egypt ✿✿✿✿✿✿✿✿✿✿✿✿✿✿✿✿✿✿✿✿✿✿

As the Mesopotamian epic of Gilgamesh reflects some of the basic viewpoints of that land, so the vast pyramids of Gizeh (just outside modern Cairo) are symbolic of early Egyptian civilization. The most mammoth of these monuments, the pyramid of Khufu (about 2600 B.C.), contains almost 6 million tons of stone in a structure 486 feet high. The rock base of the pyramid does not vary in elevation more than half an inch; its sides are almost precisely aligned with the points of the compass. The stones were very skillfully dressed for perfect fits. Construction of the pyramid together with its chapel in the valley, causeway, and funerary temple must have taken thousands of men years of work with barges, sledges, levers, and rollers. All this, in order to safeguard the actual corpse of the king so that he could protect his land after death as he did in life.

Unlike Mesopotamia, where the priests were initially most powerful, the king in Egypt was the overpowering focus of earthly life; only in the New Kingdom did the priests challenge his position. The Egyptians felt that outsiders were essentially barbarians and that their own land was designed to be a unified country. The peasants were registered in careful censuses and yielded their surplus in a variety of taxes and dues; but in return the king, as god on earth, assured the rise of the Nile, the prosperity of the land, and its peace and order. The pharaoh's will was thought to become reality as soon as he had spoken. Partly for this reason Egypt never developed the written law-codes of Mesopotamia, but the royal word was one which incarnated *ma'at* or justice. To unify itself, in other words, Egypt took the intellectually simple approach of raising its ruler to the position of a superhuman symbol but in human form.

Egyptian Religion ✿✿✿✿✿✿✿✿✿✿✿✿✿✿✿✿✿✿✿✿✿✿✿

The religion of Egypt remained always a medley of so many concepts, which themselves changed over the centuries, that it is not easily defined. Each nome or local district had a sacred totem, often in the form of an animal, and in times of unrest the nomes fought each other as bitterly in the name of these patron deities as did the Mesopotamian city-states. Higher yet stood a range of greater gods, who were conceived in animal as well as human shapes. The visible world had been created out of a watery waste by divine forces, who had also brought the gods into existence; and the gods governed all

On the right is a pharaoh of the Middle Kingdom with the crown of lower Egypt. He is escorted by the god Atum and is being given the breath of life by means of the sacred symbol called *ankh*. On the left is the god Amen. At the top of the stone are a vulture and a falcon, each with an *ankh*.

The hieroglyphs are a beautiful illustration of the pictorial character of Egyptian writing. They describe the scene and give prayers for the well-being of the pharaoh; within an oval cartouche the name of the ruler (Sesostris) is given twice.

Here, as elsewhere in Egyptian art, the heads are in profile, the torso in front view, and the legs again in profile.

aspects of human life no less than did the similar deities of Mesopotamia.

One of these great gods was Ptah of Memphis, whose priests created a story that he had formed the world. The sky was worshipped as Horus, who was a soaring falcon at times, and in a yet different concept was the son of Osiris; yet the sky could also be visualized mythologically as a cow, an ocean, a woman, and in other ways. The sun-disk came to be known principally as Re or, from the Middle Kingdom onwards, as Amen-Re. By the time of the New Kingdom this god, called Amen in shorter form, became steadily more powerful as a combination of the forces of nature. But a host of other deities populated the Egyptian mind.

Within the common polytheistic framework there were marked differences between Egypt and Mesopotamia. The gods who watched over the land of the Nile were placed in a far more cheerful light. While the lot of the Egyptian farmer was one of hard work, his life was considerably more secure than was that of a Mesopotamian peasant; and the Egyptian outlook had a tone of confidence and even enjoyment in life which was quite rare in Babylon. Each day ancient Egyptians celebrated the rebirth of the sun in the east, God's land, and watched with sorrow its disappearance in the land of the dead to the west. Each year came a great festival, the rebirth of life, as the Nile flooded and gave water and new fertility to their fields.

Afterlife

These festivals suggest another fascinating difference between Egyptian and Mesopotamian religious views, in their concepts of afterlife. In Mesopotamia, men served the gods in this life but, once dead, had only a shadowy existence. The Egyptian, on the other hand, had a very complex picture of the human soul. Accordingly he buried his dead carefully along the edge of the western desert and gradually developed detailed, graphic views of their afterlife. Such an emphasis does not mean that the inhabitants of the Nile valley were morbid, though religious fears did exist and became more pronounced by the time of the New Kingdom. The upper classes at least enjoyed life so much that they wished to cling to its delights, even after death. The inscriptions and pictures on the walls and the rich physical equipment buried in the tombs were designed in large part to achieve this aim.

At the beginning of history the god who conducted the dead to the next world was Anubis, who was visualized as a jackal-headed god. During the Old Kingdom the cult of Osiris expanded. Osiris was a legendary king, who seems to have been an embodiment of the forces of agriculture; as often happened elsewhere in the ancient Near East the fertility cults connected with farming led men on to interlinked concepts of afterlife for themselves.

In the early form of his myth, Osiris was killed by his wicked brother Seth—who at times symbolized the desert—and his corpse thrown in the Nile. His wife Isis rescued and resuscitated him temporarily so that he might sire a child by her; this was Horus, who eventually secured a trial of Seth and became king in Egypt. Osiris passed to the underworld where he was ruler and admitted the dead to his realm after testing their conduct during life on earth. In the New Kingdom he is shown at times as weighing the soul of a dead man against a feather to see if it were light enough of earthly misdeeds.

Literature and the Sciences

The arts of Egypt are justly famous and deserve special consideration (see pp. 122-29). In most intellectual fields, however, Egypt was far behind Mesopotamia.

Having evolved the symbolic meaning of the pharaoh as protector of human existence, the practical Egyptians did not feel so keenly as did the Babylonians the need to brood on the nature of the gods and the meaning of life or to fashion heroes as mediators between the divine and human planes. The heroic figure of Gilgamesh could never have arisen in the land of the Nile, which did not create any significant myths or epics to illuminate the place of man. Beyond magical incantations and praises of the ruler, which were only semi-historical, Egyptian literature consisted of travelers' tales, little stories, and manuals of advice on getting ahead in the world.

Egyptian sciences, too, remained on a practical, comparatively simple level. To Egypt we owe a solar calendar of 365 days, which perhaps crystallized about the beginning of the Old Kingdom proper. To 12 months of 30 days each were added 5 days at the end of each year, and the day was divided into 24 hours—the further subdivision of an hour into 60 minutes came in Greek times and was based on Mesopotamian counting by 60. Some very early papyri show that the Egyptians had considerable skill in surgery (and also

Statue of an Egyptian scribe with a papyrus on his lap. Those who could read and write formed the bureaucracy of ancient Egypt.

used magical spells to cure the ill). In mathematics and other areas, on the other hand, Mesopotamia was far more advanced; and such a practical invention as wheeled vehicles was not used in Egypt until the New Kingdom.

The New Kingdom

In some respects the picture of Egyptian civilization which has just been drawn fits best the naïve self-confidence of the Old Kingdom, which could erect its great pyramids as "acts of faith" to safeguard the bodies of the dead rulers. The sad fact that even such masses of stone could not protect their residents from grave robbers may suggest that not all was perfect in the land of the Nile. There were repeated periods of breakdown, and the records of the Middle Kingdom contain a good deal of complaint about injustice and exploitation. One story of this period, the tale of the Eloquent Peasant, recounts how a peasant was mistreated by a bureaucrat but insistently and successfully sought redress for his wrongs.

At the end of the Middle Kingdom invaders from Syria and Palestine, called the Hyksos, used horse-drawn chariots to conquer much of Egypt. After their expulsion and the reunification of Egypt in the New Kingdom the Egyptian kings took the initiative by invading and conquering much of Palestine and Syria. The first great conqueror in this district, Thutmose I (1528-1510 B.C.), set up a tablet of victory on the banks of the Euphrates and proclaimed in the Osiris temple at Abydos, "I have increased the work of others, the kings who have been before me; the gods had joy in my time, their temples were in festivity. I made the boundaries of Egypt as far as that which the sun encircles . . . I made Egypt the superior of every land."

Then followed a period which interests modern historians greatly, for his daughter Hatshepsut gained power and ruled Egypt from 1490 to 1468 B.C. During her reign Egypt did not engage in foreign conquests but did send an expedition down the Red Sea to gain ivory and other luxuries; scenes from this venture are portrayed in reliefs on her funerary temple at Deir el-Bahri, one of the greatest monuments of the New Kingdom.

In reality Hatshepsut was keeping the true heir, her stepson Thutmose III, out of control; on her death (natural or otherwise) he savagely erased her name from inscriptions and broke up her

The statue of queen Hatshepsut is from Deir el-Bahri. It was restored from the many parts into which her successor Thutmose III had it broken. Below is Thutmose III himself, wearing the crown of upper Egypt. The strong facial resemblance to his stepmother and aunt may be in part the result of artistic conventions in the period.

states. Then Thutmose III proceeded to wage war year after year in Asia. During 16 or 17 expeditions down to 1436 B.C. he consolidated Egyptian power on the Mediterranean coast of Asia.

During the height of its overseas rule Egypt was prosperous as never before. Internally there was peace, which permitted once more a full utilization of the land's resources; foreign mastery produced quantities of slaves and tribute. Upon the basis of these revenues the kings and nobles led a luxurious life, while the artisans and peasants dwelt in close-packed quarters. But the gods who safeguarded the empire were not forgotten. The main temple of Amen, patron of victory, was at Karnak, across the Nile from the capital of Thebes. Here the kings erected a huge hall, one of the most impressive architectural remains of ancient Egypt, and went on to add one structure after another. The religious complex at Karnak is perhaps the most extensive ever created in the Western world.

The funerary temple of queen Hatshepsut at Deir el-Bahri. In its succession of terraces it is one of the most impressive architectural schemes formed in ancient Egypt. Behind the cliffs lies the Valley of the Kings, in which many pharaohs of the New Kingdom were buried.

Hirmer Fotoarchiv, Munich

Akhenaten and His Son-in-law ❀❀❀❀❀❀❀❀❀❀❀❀❀❀❀❀❀❀❀❀

As the temples were expanded, so too grew the power of their priests; the pharaoh's position threatened to decline from that of god on earth to a mere agent for Amen. The great-great-grandson of Thutmose III, called Amenhotep IV on his accession in 1367 B.C., decided to oppose this danger. The young king commenced an amazing wave of reform, which spilled over from the political and religious fields into artistic and cultural revolution. Under his new name of Akhenaten he was to be the first reformer in history who can be seen with some clarity.

Much of the king's activity was intended to regain full authority from the priesthoods. As he proceeded, he made the usual discovery of reformers that any attempt to reduce the power of vested interests must lead one to ever more extreme measures. Eventually he decided to make a clean break with Amen, who had become almost *the* god of Egypt. In Amen's place he set up the sundisk, Aten; the hymns in Aten's honor that have survived emphasized the universal power of the god as a kindly, nurturing force. All over Egypt the temples of the local gods were closed, and the name of Amen was chiseled out of inscriptions. Since Thebes was committed to the worship of Amen, Akhenaten moved the capital 300 miles north to an entirely new site called Aketaten (the modern Amarna), isolated and well guarded, at which time he adopted as his own name Akhenaten, "It pleases Aten." The advisers and officials of the king were new men, soldiers and even foreigners, in place of the priests.

Alongside the political and religious upheaval of Akhenaten's reign there was also artistic innovation; the ruler himself seems deliberately to have encouraged artists to depict his thin face and shoulders, swollen stomach, and large thighs in more realistic fashion. The art of the Amarna age, as this period is now called, was fluid, naturalistic, and inclined to curved lines; color was employed with delicate brushwork and with pictorial sensitivity (see p. 130).

While Akhenaten concentrated on reform at home, the empire in Asia was lost to local rebellion, which was abetted by the Hittite kings of Asia Minor. Inside Egypt the conservative reaction against his reforms brought a quick abandonment of his new capital after his death in 1350 B.C. His son-in-law Tutankhamen (1347-1339 B.C.) reverted to the worship of Amen, as his name indicates, but ruled only briefly. His body was laid, like those of many other pharaohs, in the desert Valley of the Kings west of Thebes.

The great hall of the temple to Amen at Karnak. Fifty men can stand on the top of one of the capitals; the columns are over 70 feet high.

Unlike the tombs of greater kings, however, grave robbers never succeeded in looting the tomb of Tutankhamen, though they seem to have made an effort. In the 1920's Howard Carter and Lord Carnarvon had the great fortune of discovering the tomb and carefully drew out its tremendous quantity of gold, inlaid furniture, and other luxuries. If a minor pharaoh was equipped with such wealth for the next world, one can hardly imagine what originally lay in the tomb-chamber of the great conqueror Thutmose III.

Collapse of the Near East

The history of the Near East in the centuries of the 2d millennium B.C., from Hammurapi through the Egyptian New Kingdom, is a very complex story. Many countries and peoples, some of which have not even been mentioned here, entered into war and diplomacy. At Amarna excavators made a lucky find in 1887 of a mass of Egyptian state archives containing cuneiform tablets with letters from many kings, in which the foreign rulers call the Egyptian pharaoh their "brother," seek wives from his family or dispatch their own women to his harem, and urge that he "send gold in very great quantity which cannot be counted . . . For in my brother's land gold is as common as dust."

The end result of this lengthy international rivalry was the weakening of all the major states in the Near East. Their monarchs failed to notice until too late that new threats of invasion were mounting. From the desert Semitic-speaking tribes moved in about the strong-points of the cities; from the north a terrific assault broke forth in the late 13th century B.C. At least some of these invaders spoke Indo-European languages and presumably came from the great plains of Eurasia; but in the course of their advance they set many other tribes in motion. In some areas, including Asia Minor and Greece, the civilized states which had existed in the 2d millennium B.C. were wiped out. Many Syrian cities were burned and destroyed forever. The oldest centers of civilization in Egypt and Mesopotamia barely rode out the storm, but were seriously weakened.

Years B.C.	Mesopotamia	Egypt
4000	Farming villages	Farming villages
3500	Writing/cities **Sumerian domination**	
3200	Ideograms/phonograms	
3100		United kingdom **Protodynastic era**
2700		**Old Kingdom**
2600	**Akkadian domination** Sargon	Khufu △△
2300	Naram-Sin	
2100		**Middle Kingdom**
1800	**Babylonian domination** Hammurapi Venus observations	
1600	**Kassite domination**	**New Kingdom** Thutmose I Hatshepsut Thutmose III Akhenaten Tutankhamen
1300	First Assyrian empire	
1200	✵ INVADERS FROM NORTH AND DESERT	✵

End of an Era

Even in those areas which clung to civilization the period from 1200 to 900 B.C. is a dim and dreary one. The kings, warlords, and priests could no longer erect great buildings and patronize the arts. Earlier there had been preliminary tendencies to link together the main parts of the Near East economically and culturally; now life was concentrated in tiny, local units.

Every so often civilization seems to work itself into a corner from which further progress is virtually impossible along the lines then apparent. If new ideas are to have a chance the old systems of thought must be so severely shaken that they lose their dominance. Two such major collapses occurred in ancient times, one at the end of the Roman Empire in western Europe during the 5th century after Christ, the other at the end of the 2d millennium B.C. In these dismal periods many areas reverted to the food-raising stage of agricultural villages as the civilized superstructure was destroyed; yet the experience of both eras would suggest that civilization is a tough, enduring pattern of human life. Men did not everywhere abandon the major concepts which made them civilized, and when conditions became more stable they proceeded to advance on new lines—which were yet firmly grounded on the inheritance of the past.

Mesopotamian Art

The Arts of Egypt

MESOPOTAMIAN ART

History is interested especially in the thoughts and acts of people, but our first impressions of any civilization are likely to come from things which can be seen in pictures. Paris, for example, brings to mind the Eiffel Tower; Rome, the great square of Saint Peter's; and so on. If we turn back to man's first civilizations, the remains of their buildings and works of art will immediately suggest how different a spirit they represent from that which we know today.

This difference is particularly evident if we look briefly at the arts in early Mesopotamia. The lower regions along the great rivers, Sumer and Akkad, did not have good stone easily available, so the Sumerians built in brick, either baked or mud-brick. Such a material resulted in heavy, massive architecture, in which true arches were used for the first time in history. To vary the ugly brick surfaces of their temples the Sumerians recessed parts of the façade and added semi-columns on other parts; they also rammed colored terra-cotta cones into the walls to form abstract decorations. Mesopotamian temples grew larger over the centuries, but they never developed into great works of architecture.

The gods who were worshipped in these temples were visualized in human shape and were represented in statues which were essentially the gods themselves. In some temples the rulers placed before the gods statues of themselves which illustrated their piety in an equally straightforward, factual, yet reverent manner. Sometimes these statues strike

An offering stand from the Royal Cemetery at Ur, composed of a golden tree and a ram built up of shell, lapis lazuli, gold, and silver set in bitumen on a wooden body. The work shows the skill and complexity of Mesopotamian artists at their best.

Bronze head of Sargon, found at the
later Assyrian capital of Nineveh.
The eyes, in precious stones,
were gouged out, but the delicate
treatment of the hair and
diadem is still magnificent.

us as very smug, and there are amazing variations in Mesopotamian
sculptural styles over the centuries, in contrast to the basic uniformity
of Egyptian art.

As one scholar has observed, Mesopotamians generally thought of
the human form in terms of a cylinder or cone (see the stele of Naram-

Gold helmet of Meskalamdug, also found in the Royal Cemetery at Ur.

Sin on p. 87) whereas Egyptians thought in terms of a cube. Although some Mesopotamian sculptors conceived their works sharply, they did not have an intense interest in nature or a sense of human individuality. A ruler usually is an "ideal" ruler, not one specific person.

Probably the greatest achievements of Mesopotamian artists were in working metals. Many of their technical skills in handling thin gold plate or inlaying stones into metal were borrowed by later craftsmen.

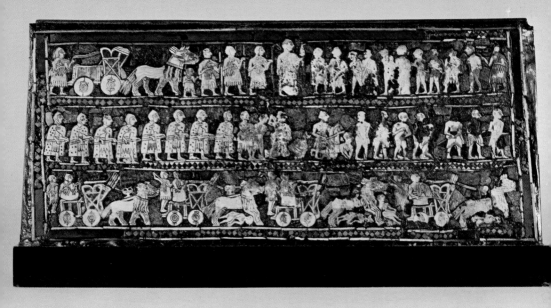

The "standard of Ur," from the Royal Cemetery, is inlaid with scenes of war and the feasting after victory. Above are soldiers and war chariots (the latter shown for the first time); below are bearers of booty and the victors at a banquet.

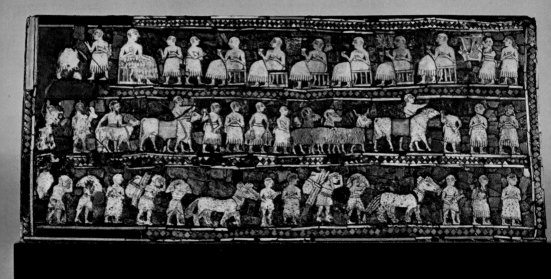

Unfortunately gold and bronze objects were usually melted down in subsequent ages to provide raw material for new creations, but archeologists have made some remarkable finds. One of the greatest is the Royal Cemetery at Ur, where a queen, her attendants, horses, and wagons were buried about 2500 B.C. in great pomp with a wealth of delicate jewelry and other luxuries.

In making seals out of metal or, more often, stone, Mesopotamian carvers also became very skillful and created a great variety of representations of animals, plants, and imaginary monsters (for an example see p. 90). Any modern student who looks at a wide sample of Mesopotamian seals will feel that this was a very different world, filled with fantasies and fears.

THE ARTS OF EGYPT

Thanks especially to the tombs of Egypt we can see more intimately into the ways of life and equipment of the Egyptians than of almost any other ancient people. The inscriptions which march across the limestone walls of noble tombs often explain or are illustrated by several rows of pictures in lightly raised relief, accentuated by color. Peasants till the fields and harvest their ample crops; nobles hunt and fish; flocks of animals and vases loaded with food abound; feasts are depicted in graphic detail. Comical scenes, even jokes appear. The purpose of this work, however, was a mixture of magic and religion; the pictures were to provide the dead with a view of human life and with earthly luxuries in the next world.

Inside the tombs were buried furniture, vases, game-boards, jewelry, servant figurines, and a host of luxurious items. These were made from the hardest of stone, from ivory, from glass, and from many other substances by patient workmen who knew a host of skillful techniques. The patterns are graceful, delicate, and also repeated over many centuries.

True sculpture appears in the statues of the dead. Since these figures were believed to contain some part of the soul of the departed and were so placed as to "receive" the food and drink offered to the dead, sculptors often worked in very hard, lasting types of stone as well as in more easily carved wood. The face of the subject was shown in a realistic fashion, but the general intent was to incarnate the dead man in a

The greatest Egyptian sculpture was carved in the Old Kingdom. Rehotep was probably the brother of king Khufu, who built the largest of the great pyramids; his wife Nofret (meaning the "good" or "beautiful") wears a wig. Egyptian artists usually painted women creamy yellow and men light to dark brown.

Female dancers and musicians from a tomb of the New Kingdom. On their heads are lumps of myrrh, which melted and provided a pleasant aroma. Other tomb reliefs and paintings will be found on pp. 43 and 50.

Hirmer Fotoarchiv, Munich

The back panel of the throne of king Tutankhamen. The scene is the hall of his palace his queen Nefertiti has a lofty crown of feathers. Above, the sun disk casts down its life-giving rays, which end in hands.

The tombs of wealthy Egyptians were equipped with a great variety of models of boats, farm animals, and other objects and also with figurines. Here is a group of Nubian archers from the Middle Kingdom; other servant figurines will be found on pp. 43 and 67.

Federico Borromeo/Scala

static pose which would reflect a quality of eternal security. Some of the greatest Egyptian sculpture came very early, before society had set that pattern of rigid conventions which dominated all later Egyptian arts. The sculptors were, on the whole, far more interested in the physical world and in reality than Sumerian artists ever dreamed of being.

Even in the best work very primitive views still reflect that limited amount of abstract analysis which one finds elsewhere in Egyptian civilization. Bodies are stiffly posed in standing or seated positions. In reliefs the lower body is shown in side view, the torso is turned frontally, and the head is in profile. The imagination of Egyptian artists was of a very matter-of-fact type.

We do not know much about Egyptian palaces and homes, which were constructed in mud-brick. Temples, however, were built largely out of stone, which could be easily quarried at many places close to the Nile and then floated down to the building site. By and large Egyptian architecture always remained most impressive for its size. Over-all planning was haphazard or even absent; working of the stone was not as finely detailed as it was to be in Greek temples. Modern excavators have often been surprised to find how flimsy are the foundations of great Egyptian buildings. In a land where rain fell often these temples would not still be standing as they are today.

A pharaoh and his wife from the Old Kingdom, a superb illustration of the serenity and quiet certainty of Egyptian art before it became conventionalized.

Whether seen from the ground or from the air, the great pyramids of Gizeh are an impressive illustration of the ability of the kings of Egypt to harness the resources of their realm.

THE ARTS OF EGYPT   127

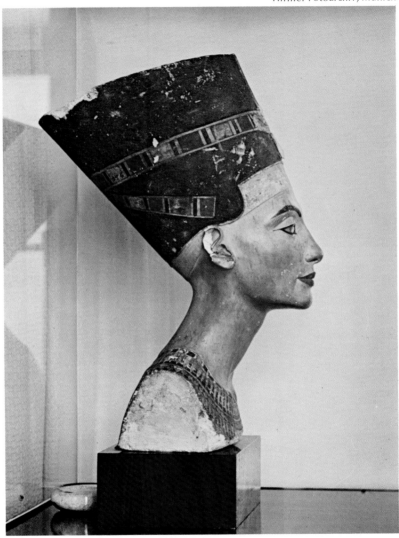

Bust of Nefertiti, probably the single most famous Egyptian sculpture. Yet it was simply a model, which was discovered at Akhetaten in the workshop of the sculptor Thutmose.

A pharaoh of the New Kingdom, standing before the god Thoth, who is giving the ruler the breath of life by means of the *ankh*. Thoth has the head of a bird, an ibis, and holds staffs which end in the crowns of upper and lower Egypt. The pharaoh has a crook-shaped scepter and a flail, the symbols of the god Osiris. The low relief is very skillfully heightened by the use of color.

If one looks carefully at the illustrations in these pages, the differences between Mesopotamian and Egyptian arts will be evident. Every area which has risen to the level of civilization has had an outlook of its own. On the other hand a modern person will feel that the arts and architecture of these earliest civilizations have fundamental similarities which distinguish them from the ways we build, paint, and carve today.

In some respects Egyptians and Mesopotamians can be called primitive, but one must always keep in mind the fact that they were trying to express a very different view about life from ours. The important point is that, as soon as men became civilized, they began to build monumentally (rather than just huts) and to carve and paint in a deliberate fashion. Their products are often still impressive even though we judge the heads of Sargon and Nefertiti by very different artistic standards.

The peculiar shape of Akhenaten's head and chest may reflect physical deformities, but the portrait is also intended as a reaction against the old conventions of Egyptian art.

SOURCES ON
MESOPOTAMIAN CIVILIZATION

We cannot listen to prehistoric men. All that the student of their history can do is to look at the physical remains of their life and speculate what these tools, paintings, and bones may mean. Once men began to write, however, the historian can hope to enter into their minds. This is not easy. Each of us today finds it hard at times to understand his friends; how much more difficult is it to put ourselves within the skin of an ancient Mesopotamian! Still, he was a man, even though he spoke a different language and worshipped different gods.

Only a very small group of devoted scholars can read cuneiform tablets. In 1835-37 and 1847 Henry Rawlinson and his assistants copied the most famous Persian inscription, carved in Old Persian, Elamite, and Babylonian parallel versions on a rock cliff at Bisutun (see p. 183), and helped to provide a key for deciphering cuneiform scripts. Semitic languages such as Assyrian, Babylonian, and Akkadian have been read for over a century; but the much more difficult Sumerian tablets have only been understood (and not always completely) for the past half-century. Nonetheless a great deal has been translated into English, and these original documents give us a sense of real life.

"Sources," as such documents are called, are extremely valuable, but the historian is as cautious in assessing their truth as is any detective. In using sources the historian must always try to determine when and where they were written and who their author was. Only thus can the student of history answer questions such as: Could the writer have known this? Is his report second-hand? What prejudices of social class, religion, etc. does he share? If a writer says so-and-so many enemy were killed, is he trying to flatter the victor? Does he give the real causes of an event?

In the following pages some Mesopotamian sources (originally in Sumerian or Babylonian) are quoted so that the reader can listen to the voices of men and women from the days of Hammurapi and earlier.

A. THE GODS

The view which men have of their gods in any age reveals much about the fundamental characteristics and forms of their society. In these passages one may gain light as to whether Mesopotamian men thought the gods lovable or all-powerful, and how men could gain their favor.

By chance we have not only the poem of Enheduanna but also a representation of her on a battered limestone disk from Ur, with a servant before her.

University Museum,
University of Pennsylvania

1. The Prayer of Enheduanna

The earliest writer in human history of whom we know the name is Enheduanna, daughter of the great Sargon of Agade, who was appointed high priestess of the main temple of Ur in the 24th century B.C. She wrote a hymn in praise of Ishtar (called Inanna in Sumerian), which celebrates the power of the goddess in love and war. Two stanzas are as follows:

Destroyer of the foreign lands, you have given wings to the storm,
Beloved of Enlil you made it blow over the land,
You carried out the instructions of An.
My queen, the foreign lands cower at your cry,
In dread (and) fear of the South Wind, mankind
Brought you their anguished clamor,
Took before you their anguished outcry
Opened before you wailing and weeping,
Brought before you the "great" lamentations in the city streets.

The mountain who kept from paying homage to you—vegetation became "tabu" for it,
You burnt down its great gates,
Its rivers ran with blood because of you, its people had nothing to drink,
Its troops were led off willingly (into captivity) before you,
Its forces disbanded themselves willingly before you,
Its strong men paraded willingly before you,
The amusement places of its cities were filled with turbulence,
Its adult males were driven off as captives before you.

2. Hymn to Ishtar

Dating about 1600 B.C., this hymn presents Ishtar in a different light:

She is clothed with pleasure and love.
She is laden with vitality, charm, and voluptuousness.
Ishtar is clothed with pleasure and love.
She is laden with vitality, charm, and voluptuousness.

In lips she is sweet; life is in her mouth.
At her appearance rejoicing becomes full.
She is glorious; veils are thrown over her head.
Her figure is beautiful; her eyes are brilliant.

She dwells in, she pays heed to compassion and friendliness.
Besides, agreeableness she truly possesses.
Be it slave, unattached girl, or mother, she preserves her.
One calls on her; among women one names her name.

Who—to her greatness can be equal?
Strong, exalted, splendid are her decrees.
Ishtar—to her greatness who can be equal?
Strong, exalted, splendid are her decrees.

3. The Curse of Agade

As in the Old Testament, historical events were considered by the Mesopotamians to be the result of divine action. Naram-Sin of Agade, the grandson of Sargon, first ruled happily but then destroyed the temple called Ekur at Nippur, the sacred city of the Sumerians. The gods impelled mountaineers from the east to wipe out Agade. The first selection shows the prosperity of the city, the second gives the curse of the gods:

In those days the dwellings of Agade were filled with gold,
Its bright-shining houses were filled with silver,
Into its granaries were brought copper, lead, and slabs of lapis lazuli,
Its silos bulged at the sides,
Its old women were endowed with counsel,
Its old men were endowed with eloquence,
Its young men were endowed with the "strength of weapons,"
Its little children were endowed with joyous hearts,
Its quay where the boats docked were all abustle,
All lands lived in security,
Their people witnessed (nothing but) happiness,
Their king Naram-Sin, the shepherd,
Stepped forward like the sun on the holy dais of Agade,
Its walls reached skyward like a mountain.

.   .   .

"City, you who dared assault the Ekur—it is Enlil (whom you assaulted),
Agade, you who dared assault the Ekur—it is Enlil (whom you assaulted),
At your holy wall, lofty as it is, may wailing resound,
May your wrestler rejoice not in his strength, may he lie in darkness,
May famine kill (the people of) that city,
May the princely children who ate (only) the very best bread, lie
    about in the grass,
May your man who used to carry off the first fruits, eat the scraps
    of his tables,
The leather thongs of the door of his father's house,
May he munch these leather thongs with his teeth;

May your palace built in joy, fall to ruins in anguish . . .
Agade (instead of) your sweet-flowing water, may salt water flow there,
May he who said 'I would sleep in that city,' not find a good
  dwelling there,
May he who said, 'I would sleep in Agade,' not find a good sleeping
  place there."
And lo, with Utu's bringing forth the day, so it came to pass!
Agade is destroyed! Praise Inanna.

4. Atrahasis

A famous Babylonian tale described the creation of mankind, the
sending of a flood by the gods, and the survival of Atrahasis ("Ex-
ceedingly Wise") with his family in an ark:

> The land became wide, the people became numerous,
> The land bellowed like wild oxen.
> The god was disturbed by their uproar.
> Enlil heard their clamor
> And said to the great gods:
> "Oppressive has become the clamor of mankind.
> By their uproar they prevent sleep.
> Let the fig be cut off for the people,
> In their bellies let the greens be too few.
> Above let Adad make scarce his rain,
> Below let not flow
> The flood, let it not rise from the source."

After a period when all growth stopped and men turned to cannibalism, there came the Flood; but first Atrahasis was commanded to
build a large ship, into which he was to take the beasts of the field
and the fowl of the heavens. Atrahasis had to ask the god Ea to
draw him a plan of such a ship, and then he constructed it. The
story of the actual Flood is not preserved in our Atrahasis tablets,
but it turns up also in the epic of Gilgamesh where the hero Ut-
napishtim is the builder of the ark. He survived seven days of flood
and wind:

> When the seventh day arrived,
> The sea grew quiet, the tempest was still, the flood ceased.
> I looked at the weather: stillness had set in,
> And all of mankind had returned to clay.

The landscape was as level as a flat roof.
I opened a hatch, and light fell upon my face.
Bowing low, I sat and wept,
Tears running down on my face.

His ark grounded on Mount Nisir, and he sent forth in turn a dove, a swallow, and then a raven before the waters receded enough for earth to reappear. Then Ut-napishtim could pour a libation for the gods and leave his ark.

5. The Virtue of Prayer

One of the oldest known examples of Mesopotamian literature, the Instructions of Shuruppak (which existed before 2500 B.C.), is a collection of practical advice to a son, not to loiter where there is a dispute or to speak ill of others but to be friendly to one's enemy. One stanza deals with the gods:

Worship your god every day.
Sacrifice and pious utterance are the proper accompaniment of
    incense.
Have a freewill offering for your god,
For this is proper toward a god.
Prayer, supplication, and prostration
Offer him daily, then your prayer will be granted,
And you will be in harmony with your god.

B. MEN AND WOMEN

1. The King

A Mesopotamian proverb, "Man is the shadow of a god, and a slave is the shadow of a man; but the king is the mirror of a god." We have already seen the efforts of Hammurapi to assure justice; an earlier Sumerian king, Shulgi, boasted:

Like my heroship, like my might,
I am accomplished in wisdom as well,
I vie with its [wisdom's] true word,
I love justice,
I do not love evil,
I hate the evil word,
I, Shulgi, a mighty king, supreme, am I.
Because I am a powerful man rejoicing in his "loins,"
I enlarged the footpaths, straightened the highways of the land,
I made secure travel, built there "big houses,"

Planted gardens alongside of them, established resting-places,
Settled there friendly folk,
So that who comes from below, who comes from above,
Might refresh themselves in its cool shade.

As a historian, how far would you believe this statement?

2. The Duty of Man

One person whom Gilgamesh met in his search for everlasting life to restore Enkidu advised him:

Gilgamesh, whither rovest thou?
The life thou pursuest thou shalt not find.
When the gods created mankind,
Death for mankind they set aside,
Life in their own hands retaining.
Thou, Gilgamesh, let full be thy belly,
Make thou merry by day and by night.
Of each day make thou a feast of rejoicing,
Day and night dance thou and play!
Let thy garments be sparkling fresh,
Thy head be washed; bathe thou in water.
Pay heed to the little one that holds on to thy hand,
Let thy spouse delight in thy bosom!
For this is the task of mankind!

3. The Troubles of Man

Not all family life was as serene as suggested in the last lines above. The son of one of Hammurapi's governors wrote to his mother in a letter full of mistakes in the script:

Gentlemen's clothes improve year by year. You are the one making my clothes cheaper year by year. By cheapening and scrimping my clothes you have become rich. The son of Adad-iddinam, whose father is only an underling of my father, has received two new garments, but you keep getting upset over just one garment for me. Whereas you gave birth to me, his mother acquired him by adoption, but whereas his mother loves him, you do not love me.

In a legend of the love of Ishtar (Inanna) and the god Tammuz, Ishtar complains she does not know what she will tell her mother to excuse her absence that night. Tammuz replies:

"Let me inform you, let me inform you.
Inanna, most deceitful of women, let me inform you:

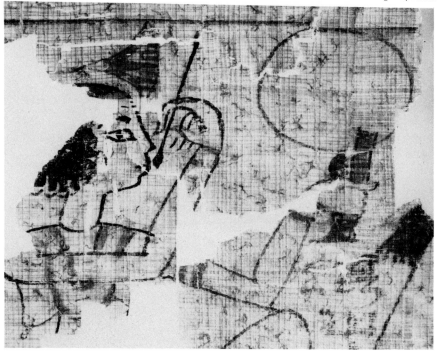

An Egyptian girl rouging her lips while holding a mirror in her other hand. Feminine wiles are not exactly new in history.

'My girl friend took me with her to the public square,
She entertained me there with music and dancing,
Her chant, the sweet, she sang for me.
In sweet rejoicing I whiled away the time there'—
Thus deceitfully stand up to your mother,
While we by the moonlight indulge our passion."

Laws also reveal much of social conditions. To give some provisions of the code of Hammurapi:

If outlaws have congregated in the establishment of a woman wine seller and she has not arrested those outlaws and did not take them to the palace, that wine seller shall be put to death.

If an obligation came due against a free man and he sold the services of his wife, his son, or his daughter, or he has been bound over to service, they shall work in the house of their purchaser or obligee for three years, with their freedom reestablished in the fourth year.

If a free man acquired a wife, but did not draw up the contracts for her, that woman is no wife.

If a free man wishes to divorce his wife who did not bear him children, he shall give her money to the full amount of her marriage-price and he shall also make good to her the dowry which she brought from her father's house and then he may divorce her.

If there was no marriage-price, he shall give her one mina of silver as the divorce-settlement.

If he is a peasant, he shall give her one-third mina of silver.

If a free man's wife, who was living in the house of the free man, has made up her mind to leave in order that she may engage in business, thus neglecting her house and humiliating her husband, they shall prove it against her; and if her husband has then decided on her divorce, he may divorce her, with nothing to be given her as her divorce-settlement upon her departure.

If a woman so hated her husband that she has declared, "You may not have me," her record shall be investigated at her city council, and if she was careful and was not at fault, that woman, without incurring any blame at all, may take her dowry and go off to her father's house.

If she was not careful, but was a gadabout, thus neglecting her house and humiliating her husband, they shall throw that woman into the water.

If a free man, having made up his mind to disinherit his son, has said to the judges, "I wish to disinherit my son," the judges shall investigate his record, and if the son did not incur wrong grave enough to cut him off from sonship, the father may not cut his son off from sonship.

If he has incurred wrong against his father grave enough to cut him off from sonship, they shall condone his first offense; if he has incurred grave wrong a second time, the father may cut off his son from sonship.

If a member of the artisan class took a son as a foster child and has taught him his handicraft, he may never be reclaimed.

If he has not taught him his handicraft, that foster child may return to his father's house.

If a free man, who adopted a boy and reared him, set up a family of his own, has later acquired children and so has made up his mind to cut off the foster child, that son shall not go off empty-handed; his foster father shall give him from his goods his one-third patrimony, and then he shall go off, since he may not give him any of the field, orchard, or house.

An actual adoption contract of the period of Hammurapi runs:

> Yahatti-el is the son of Hillalum and Alitum. He shall rejoice in their joys and commiserate in their miseries. Should Hillalum, his father, and Alitum, his mother, ever say to their son Yahatti-el: "You are not our son," they shall forfeit house and belongings. Should Yahatti-el say to Hillalum, his father, and to Alitum, his mother: "You are not my father; you are not my mother," they shall have him shaved, and shall sell him for money. As for Hillalum and Alitum—regardless of how many sons they shall have acquired—Yahatti-el is primary heir, and he shall take a double share of the estate of Hillalum, his father. His younger brothers shall divide the remainder in equal shares.

4. Foretelling

In so troubled a world men needed to have ways by which they could appease their gods and also find out the future. The technique of casting horoscopes which appears in modern newspapers did not

Another means of foretelling the future was to slaughter an animal and examine its internal organs (especially the liver). Any unusual color or shape had its special significance in giving an indication of the will of the gods. This clay model is divided into sections, each of which is described in cuneiform script.

British Museum

yet exist, but celestial events could be interpreted for the benefit of the kings. There was a great variety of other means of exploring what was to happen to a man; in Mesopotamian literature, thus, an extended body of dream-interpretation was built up. Here are some quotable examples:

> If, in his dreams, he often walks about naked it means: trouble will not touch this man.
> If a man flies repeatedly: whatever he owns will be lost.
> If a man carries a sprout and kisses it repeatedly: this man will acquire barley and silver. But if it grows out of his lap: whatever he owns will be lost.
> If he sits on the ground: honors are in store for him.
> If he pours his urine into an irrigation-canal: Adad (the Weather-god) will flood his harvest.
> If he goes to Lagash: he will be robbed.
> If he goes to set a wood-pile afire: he will see days of sadness.
> If he eats the eye of his friend: his bad luck is straightened out, his property will prosper.
> If one gives him a seal of red stone: he will have sons and daughters.
> If one gives him a wheel: he will have twins.
> If one gives him wine: his days will be short.

Occasionally the diagnosis of the meaning of the dream is more rational than it may appear at first glance; wheels, for instance, usually came in pairs. In other cases the dreams are similar to those discussed by Freud and other modern analysts, but the explanations are of a different order. Mesopotamian men, however, evidently worried and dreamed as much as have those in more recent ages.

PART III

Empires and Subjects

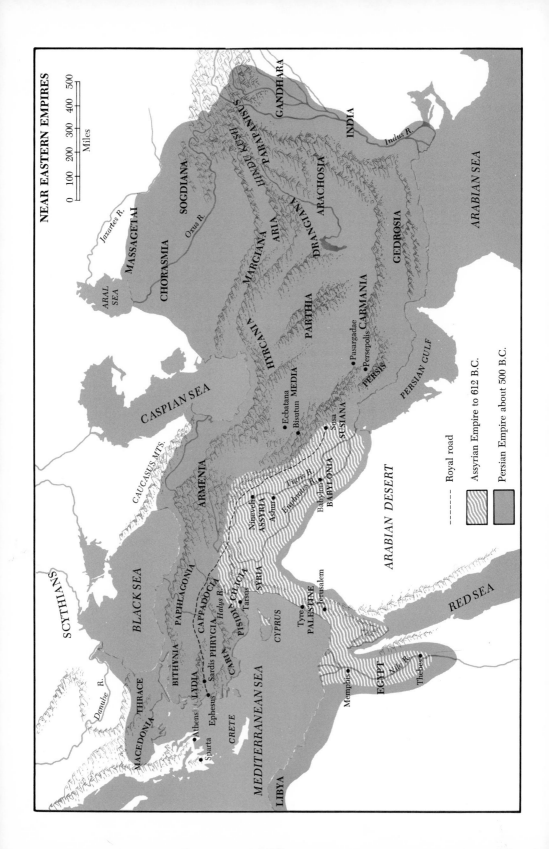

NEAR EASTERN EMPIRES

0 100 200 300 400 500
Miles

- - - - Royal road

Assyrian Empire to 612 B.C.

Persian Empire about 500 B.C.

SCYTHIANS

MASSAGETAI

CHORASMIA

SOGDIANA

GANDHARA

PARAPANISUS

HINDU KUSH

INDIA

Indus R.

ARABIAN SEA

Jaxartes R.

Oxus R.

ARAL SEA

ARIA

MARGIANA

ARACHOSIA

DRANGIANA

HYRCANIA

PARTHIA

CARMANIA

GEDROSIA

CASPIAN SEA

Ecbatana

Bisutun MEDIA

PERSIS

Pasargadae

Persepolis

PERSIAN GULF

CAUCASUS MTS.

Susa

SUSIANA

ARMENIA

Tigris R.

Nineveh

ASSYRIA

Ashur

Euphrates R.

Babylon

BABYLONIA

ARABIAN DESERT

BLACK SEA

PAPHLAGONIA

BITHYNIA

CAPPADOCIA

Halys R.

SYRIA

PISIDIA CILICIA

Tarsus

CARIA PHRYGIA

Sardis

LYDIA

Ephesus

Jerusalem

Tyre

PALESTINE

CYPRUS

RED SEA

THRACE

MACEDONIA

Athens

Sparta

CRETE

MEDITERRANEAN SEA

LIBYA

Memphis

EGYPT

Nile R.

Thebes

Danube R.

In the preceding Part we looked especially at Babylon about 1750 B.C. and also, more briefly, at the historical development of Egypt. It is time now to take a mighty leap, all the way down to 500 B.C., when the Persians had united the Near East into one empire. This Persian state stretched from the Aegean Sea eastward through modern Afghanistan, northwestern India, and Russian Turkestan.

The majesty of this great empire was symbolized by a great festival on New Year's Day, which took place at the Persian fortress-treasury of Persepolis, high in the mountains of Iran. From all the many regions of the Near East their representatives brought the Persian king his annual tribute—prize horses, fat lambs, gold vessels, incense, precious metals almost beyond measure. Lively nobles of the Persians and their kinsmen, the Medes, attended in festive attire; royal spearsmen stood stiffly in guard. The nature of the event we know largely because it was lovingly depicted on the reliefs of two staircases at Persepolis, which are in part illustrated on p. 156.

To conclude our investigation of the rise and nature of civilization we should look briefly at the Persian empire and its major predecessor, the Assyrian empire. Some of the Persian subjects, however, are important enough to deserve independent mention. Two of these, the Phoenicians and the Hebrews, are considered in Chapter 7.

CHAPTER **6**

The Assyrian and Persian Empires

Reinvigoration of the Near East ❋❋❋❋❋❋❋❋❋❋❋❋❋❋❋❋❋❋❋❋
The ancient world had been subjected to rude shocks and terrific invasions from about 1200 B.C. onwards. For almost three centuries no new palaces seem to have been erected in the Near East; written records and artistic remains alike are not extensive.

Cultural and economic ties, however, were not totally shattered, and from about 900 B.C. on the Near East recovered. Trade became ever more active, and artistic activity was resumed. Solomon had already built a palace at Jerusalem before 900 B.C. Thereafter the kings of the small Syrian kingdoms, who mostly spoke a Semitic language called Aramaic, began to live in greater pomp.

In the revival of economic activity two developments were significant alongside the spread of alphabets (which will be considered in Chapter 7). One was the wider use of the camel as a beast of burden. Although camels are mean, quarrelsome beasts, they could carry far more than could donkeys or asses; in one tariff their loads were assessed at five times that of a donkey.

Another change was the common use of iron. While iron ores can be melted and refined at a lower temperature than that required for copper, the process takes a longer time, and truly useful weapons and tools of iron involved a complicated technique of repeated heating, quenching, and hammering. Iron objects have turned up in levels of the 5th millennium B.C. (sometimes of meteoric source); smiths of the 2d millennium in Asia Minor went further in working the metal; but adequate methods of hardening iron products became commonly known only after 1000 B.C. Iron accordingly was used on a large scale only from 900 B.C. onwards.

The manufacture of bronze had been limited by periodic shortages of tin, which is a rare metal, and had been restricted largely to weapons and objects for the upper classes. Iron ores, on the other hand, occurred widely over ancient Eurasia and could be turned into tools of common use as well; in one Assyrian warehouse over 150 tons of iron ingots were discovered. Ancient techniques, which introduced a good deal of carbon, generally produced a mild steel or at times wrought iron; cast iron was uncommon. On the basis of these and other changes trade and industry across the Near East had reached unprecedented heights by 800 B.C.

Imperialism ❁❁❁❁❁❁❁❁❁❁❁❁❁❁❁❁❁❁❁❁❁❁❁❁❁❁❁

The fruit of renewed order was first the rise of petty kingdoms, which guaranteed local stability. Then came the consolidation of these units into a great territorial state or empire.

Today the word imperialism has such a bad flavor that each of the great powers calls its rivals "imperialist" as the worst possible abuse. But when the historian surveys past ages, he finds that imperialism has been very common from the great days of the British on back through Rome to the Near Eastern empires. Sargon of Agade, in the 3d millennium B.C., was the first great imperialist of whom we know; but he had many successors, Hammurapi and Thutmose III among others. Any time the student of history meets a commonly repeated pattern of events, it is his duty to try to understand why that pattern should take place—though he does not have to praise all its results.

In general terms, imperialism can be taken as meaning the rule of areas or peoples who are different in culture or languages from their masters. Modern theory usually explains its appearance as being the result of economic motives, such as the search for raw materials and for profits. This line of explanation does not always fit modern examples of imperialism, and it certainly is not adequate to account for ancient empires. True, imperial conquerors took away much of the movable wealth from those whom they defeated and demanded tribute thereafter. Yet rulers and armies alike also yearned for glory and, perhaps unconsciously at times, wished to demonstrate the power of their protecting gods and ways of life.

As soon as civilization began, the glory of kings was shown in victory. In this case the figures represent the conquest of lower Egypt and the Delta by a king from upper Egypt.

Narmer, one of the first kings of united Egypt, wears the crown of upper Egypt. With his mace he is striking a defeated enemy of the "harpoon" district. Above, to the right, the king is represented as the falcon god Horus, who is holding by the lip the head of a captive; the hieroglyph with papyrus plants means the Delta. Below the king are two fallen enemies, each with a hieroglyph representing a specific district.

Another aspect of empire must also be kept in mind: no empire lasts very long by brute force. The subjects of ancient empires had to pay their tribute, as shown in the New Year's festival at Persepolis; but if Persian rule lasted over two centuries it must have given something in return. What the subjects gained, essentially, was internal peace and protection from outside foes. In many areas, such as central Asia, they also gained the opportunity to raise themselves, in relative tranquility, to the level of civilization. The Near Eastern empires could not always prevent their subjects from desiring independence and revolting at times; but the Persians in particular were among the most successful rulers in history.

Rise of the Assyrian Empire

The predecessors of the Persians, however, in uniting the Near East were the Assyrians. If we are to explain why this particular folk rose into dominance over others, we must look both to the earlier tradition of Assyria and to its location. Assyria was a state formed about the heavily fortified city of Ashur on the middle Tigris, which had become civilized in the 3d millennium B.C. under the impetus of Mesopotamian progress. In the 2d millennium it had had a brief opportunity for external expansion, then lay quietly during the age of troubles, and began to revive about 900 B.C.

At this time it was a small kingdom scarcely more than 70 miles on a side, a region in which culture and commerce were secondary to farming, herding, and military activity. The relation of Assyria to Babylonia has often been compared to the later connection of Rome with Greece. Both Assyria and Rome were indebted to their more civilized neighbors, though neither Assyrian nor Roman culture was simply a blind copy of its model. Both Assyria and Rome, again, had a military structure in their life, born of the necessity for constant warfare against nearby hillsmen; and both had a strong sense of divine protection by their native gods. The main deity of Assyria was the sun-god, also called Ashur, for whose glory the Assyrian monarchs fought stubbornly and successfully.

Initially the kings followed the practice of raiding down the Tigris, across to the Euphrates, and then up this river to the hills, whence they returned home with loot and glory. These raids they described in detailed records or "annals" for the pleasure of Ashur. In the 8th century B.C., however, the greatest Assyrian imperialist, Tiglath-Pileser III (744-727), first seized the throne and then con-

An Assyrian king on horseback, drawing his bow to shoot wild game.

quered as far as the Mediterranean. Later rulers took Israel and even added Egypt briefly to the Assyrian empire. In all, the Near East was unified for about a century, down to the fall of the Assyrian capital of Nineveh in 612 B.C.

Organization of the Assyrian Empire ❀❀❀❀❀❀❀❀❀❀❀❀❀❀❀

Around the homeland of Assyria proper lay the dependent regions, which for the first time were organized into provinces, each with an Assyrian governor. Although powerful, the governors were closely checked by subordinates or by agents and spies from the central court. In the provinces some cities were ruled directly by Assyrian deputies; Assyrian garrisons lay in a few major fortresses. Other local kings had Assyrian "residents" to watch their behavior, and relatively safe areas were left free of such direct or indirect supervision.

The heart of the system was the Assyrian king, "the great king, the legitimate king, the king of the world, king of Assyria, king of all the four rims of the earth, king of kings, prince without rival, who rules from the Upper Sea to the Lower Sea." Most of the rulers were forceful men, who spent the campaigning season in the field; weaklings had little chance to keep the throne against ambitious relatives or outsiders. One king specially states that he was always guarded, and with good reason; for a number of the monarchs fell victim to internal plots.

To support their position the kings built up an extensive court and central bureaucracy, including a chief minister, cupbearer, chamberlain, eunuchs, and the like. Some parts of the royal archives have survived. In the petitions, diplomatic correspondence, intelligence reports, and letters one can see the careful royal supervision of the imperial administration and can sense the unending struggle to keep the subject peoples under control.

The army upon which this royal power rested was drawn initially from the Assyrian nobles and peasantry, but as this source became exhausted in continual war the kings also had to employ subject peoples and mercenaries. It was the first great army to use iron weapons, and it was well organized. The shock mobile force was the chariotry, equipped chiefly with the bow, alongside which skirmished light cavalry. The basic infantry block consisted of men with helmet, shield, spear and dagger, but light-armed infantry were also useful. The quality of any army can often be measured by its ability to traverse mountains, which are a good area for ambushes and impose severe stress on supply systems, and also by its willingness to stick to the monotonous, protracted operations of a siege with mines, rams, and towers. In both respects the Assyrian army had no equal down to its period.

Character of the Assyrian Empire

Neither at the time nor in later memory did the Assyrian empire enjoy a favorable reputation. Peace and order were purchased by its subjects at a heavy price in cash and lives, a price which is frightfully evident in the frank Assyrian records. The annals of the kings itemize jubilantly the fruits of conquest—the silver, gold, copper, iron, furniture, cattle, female slaves, and hosts of other trophies—and recount directly the brutalities inflicted on the defeated. One king boasts, "I destroyed them, tore down the walls and burned the towns with fire; I caught the survivors and impaled them on stakes in front of their towns."

Even more disturbing is the open parade of brutality and violence in the great reliefs which decorated the Assyrian palaces. Heads of conquered kings hung in the trees of the royal gardens; the human debris of battlefield and siege was graphically depicted. Often the leaders in an area which rebelled were transplanted to areas far from their homeland. At other times defeated peoples were slain by the hundreds, and their grinning skulls were piled up neatly by the roadsides to provide an object lesson for travelers.

This ruthless spirit perhaps proves not so much that the Assyrians were inhuman monsters as it shows the sternness required to break and harness the Near East. The Assyrian period was in reality one of the greatest turning points in the civilized history of the area. The next great empire, the Persian, reaped the benefit and could afford to exercise its sway in a more lenient style.

The obvious source of the Assyrian empire was the ambition of its rulers and upper classes for the glory and profit of war and perhaps their zeal to spread the sway of the sun-god Ashur; but it had also an unconscious base in economic and cultural benefits. The Assyrians provided peace and order; they also cherished the cosmopolitan Mesopotamian civilization which formed a large part of their inheritance. Like the rulers of the Roman empire in later days they fostered the spread of a consolidated pattern of artistic and intellectual life throughout their domains.

Interregnum ❈

Yet the Assyrians could not gain the loyalty of their subjects; throughout the last 50 years of their power the kings of Assyria were on the defensive. Internally the kernel of the empire, the Assyrians themselves, was destroyed by the drafts of the wars. Externally the monarchs could not maintain their control over Egypt, which was too isolated and remote to be held easily. More serious threats came from Babylonia and from the mountains of Iran, where the dynasty of the Medes was uniting the warlike inhabitants of the upland valleys. Together the Babylonians and Medians pulled down the rotten shell of Assyrian might.

Nineveh, the cosmopolitan capital, was destroyed in 612. Some of the Assyrian subjects, interestingly enough, supported the last Assyrian kings, but in vain. Far off in Judah the Hebrew prophet Nahum exulted at the news, "Woe to the bloody city! It is all full of lies and robbery . . . Nineveh is laid waste: Who will bemoan her!" Assyria had collapsed forever; within a century Nineveh had dissolved into huge mounds of ruins.

For the next half-century the Near East was divided between the Medes and Babylonians. The most famous king of the latter state, Nebuchadrezzar (605-562 B.C.), destroyed the small Hebrew kingdom of Judah and demolished the temple of Jerusalem in 586 B.C. At home Nebuchadrezzar built the fabulous Hanging Gardens (a roof garden supported by brick arches) and surrounded his capital by a double wall 10 miles long. The great Ishtar Gate on the main processional street is illustrated in some of its details on p. 177.

Beginnings of the Persian Empire (550-530 B.C.) ❈ ❈ ❈ ❈ ❈ ❈ ❈ ❈ ❈ ❈

The Persians were one of the minor tribes of Iran, located in the mountains southeast of Susa. Their royal line traced its ancestry from a man named Achaemenes (in his Greek form) and occasionally intermarried with the more powerful Median dynasty to the north; but the Achaemenids were utterly unimportant until a brilliant youth, Cyrus, ascended the throne in 559.

First Cyrus gained the support of the Iranian nobility to oust the Median king in 550. Then he struck far west to Asia Minor and overthrew Croesus of Lydia in 547. Thereafter he turned back on Babylon where Marduk, according to Cyrus' story, was "searching for a righteous ruler." This man he found in Cyrus, whom he called

The surviving columns and one of the staircases of the audience hall at Persepolis. Details of the staircase reliefs are shown in the next pictures.

"to become ruler of all the world." Babylon fell without a struggle in 539 as the priests and people refused to support their own dynasty.

Cyrus died in battle against Eurasian nomads on his northeastern frontier in 530; his son Cambyses added Egypt to the Persian empire before committing suicide in a fit of mental derangement (see p. 185). A relative of the Achaemenid line, Darius, then became king (521-486) and conquered the north coast of the Aegean, though he failed in a bold effort to acquire power over the north shore of the Black Sea.

Of all the events described in this book the swift rise of the Persians to mastery over all the Near East is the most amazing, almost miraculous. How could it have happened?

Some of the later Persian kings followed the teachings of a prophet called Zoroaster, who proclaimed an ethical faith. In Zoroastrianism the god of light and truth, Ahura Mazda, stood opposed to the evil force Ahriman. All men in the world must support the good by their deeds or else serve the spirits of darkness. But this powerful religious belief, which still survives among the Parsees of India and in some parts of Iran, cannot be used to explain the Persian onrush, for the first Persian king firmly to worship Ahura Mazda was Darius.

Rather, we must look for an explanation to the abilities of the kings themselves and the warlike temper of the Iranian nobility on the one hand, and to the fact that the Assyrians had broken the independence of the Near East on the other. Underlying the survival of Persian rule for two centuries were the cultural unity of this world and the relatively easy-going temper of Persian rule.

Organization of the Persian Empire

The Persian empire in theory was an autocracy under "the great king, king of kings, king of the countries possessing many kinds of people, king of this great earth far and wide." In sculptured reliefs the monarch looms out, sharply distinguished by his square beard cut off at the waist, dressed in tiara, purple robe, and white or crimson trousers. He sits on a high throne, with a stool to protect his feet from contact with the ground; a parasol shades his head; and a fly-flapper attends his sacred majesty.

In boastful inscriptions, including the famous Bisutun trilingual proclamation (see p. 182) by Darius, the Persian kings underlined their absolutism, their justice, and the belief that they held their powers by divine grant. In Egypt the Persian king succeeded the pharaohs and was a god on earth; in Babylon, Marduk, according to Cyrus, had sought a righteous prince and found his choice in Cyrus; among the Persians themselves Darius proclaimed that "by the grace of Ahura Mazda Darius is the king."

This divine-right monarchy was necessarily tempered in practice. Six of the great Persian noble families, which had helped Darius during the civil war, enjoyed special rights; and the Persians as a whole formed a privileged group. The nobles, in particular, were advisers, officials, and cavalry in time of war; young nobles were taught in cadet school, according to the Greek historian Herodotus, "to ride, to draw the bow and to speak the truth." Persian commoners were exempt from taxes and furnished the most solid block of heavy infantry, including the king's bodyguard of "Immortals." As garrison troops and as officials the Persians were scattered widely over the empire.

Cilicians bring their tribute of sheep to the Persian king. Below are his nobles, the Persians with fluted caps and the Medes with round caps; they have bow cases or swords and bear lotus flowers in their hands. Originally these reliefs from the east staircase at Persepolis were painted in vivid colors.

The empire itself was divided into tributary kingdoms and great provinces, called satrapies from the Median word *satrap* or governor. Under Darius each of the 20 satrapies at that time was required to yield specific quantities of tax in money, horses, and other items and provided contingents of ships or soldiers to the Persian navy and army. The satraps were virtually local kings, who often inherited their positions and had wide powers in local government and foreign affairs; but they were checked by royally appointed secretaries, garrison commanders, and traveling inspectors, called the king's "eyes and ears."

Roads radiating from the central capital of Susa and also from Ecbatana and Babylon were much improved and carried the imperial post. The most famous of these roads was the Royal road from Ephesus on the Aegean coast to Susa, a journey of three months, which was much traveled over the centuries by Greek ambassadors, merchants, learned men, and captives of war. Along these roads also traveled native traders and artists, almost all of whom used Aramaic as a common language of the Near East. Even Persian administrators tended to employ Aramaic more and more.

Persians and Greeks ❀
Far off in the northwest corner of the world—as the Persian kings looked at the map—lay some backward peoples in the poor, rocky landscape of Greece. This area, too, had suffered in the invasions from 1200 B.C. on; the kingdoms of the area, which had built palaces and used writing, had been wiped out together with all the civilized arts. In the dull, home-keeping centuries which followed, the Greeks developed the fundamental aspects of their way of life; the *Iliad* and the *Odyssey* had both been composed before 700 B.C. Then the Greeks began again to trade with the Near East, adopted and modified the Phoenician alphabet, and engaged in a great wave of colonization which deposited little nuclei of Greek civilization over much of the western Mediterranean and the Black Sea.

Throughout Assyrian times the Greeks had little political contact with the Near East and could continue to develop without facing direct pressure from Near Eastern empires. As the Persians drove across Asia Minor, however, they conquered first the Greeks of the Asia Minor coast and then those of the north Aegean. By 500 B.C. the Greek homeland lay directly under the cloud of Persian might.

Any sober calculator of odds at this point would have bet that

King Darius, with lotus flower, tiara, and staff, sits on a high throne with a footstool. Behind him the crown prince stands on the platform which bears the throne. Before the king are two incense burners and the Median commander of his bodyguard.

the huge strength of Persia would overcome the Aegean world. The Greeks too were expanding but were politically divided into very little, jealous countries such as Athens and Sparta. When the Persians did invade Greece in 480, the great Greek god Apollo from his oracle at Delphi gave no encouragement to those stubborn Greeks who resisted the majesty and blessings of Persian rule.

A Persian gold coin, called a "daric." The king is running with tiara, staff, and bow.

The Greeks, as we all know, won despite the odds. Their victory may serve as a symbol that an essentially new pattern of civilization, which we call Western, could hold its own against the Near East. Most of us would feel that the Greeks, not the Persians, are our spiritual ancestors; yet the Greeks could not have developed as they did if they had not been able to draw on the accomplishments of the Near East.

There is another point always to keep in mind. Both Persian and Greek ways of life continued to survive, and even the conquests by Alexander the Great did not wipe out the patterns of Near Eastern culture. Much, much later, in the days of the Arabs (after A.D. 600) and then the Turks, the Near East was again to be the home of even greater political and cultural power than the Persian kings had exercised.

7

The Subjects

Rulers and Subjects ✿
In the eyes of the Persian kings the inhabitants of the empire were
subjects, whose purpose was to uphold and maintain royal power.
On some doorjambs of the palaces at Persepolis the peoples of the
many provinces are represented as rows of men who support the
carved representation of the king on his throne.

A long building inscription from Susa tells of the thorough prep-
arations for the palace there by Darius. "Deep down the earth was
dug, until rock bottom I reached. When the excavation was made,
gravel was packed down, one part sixty feet, the other thirty feet
in depth." Then follows a list of the work done by each subject
people. To give one example, "the cedar timber was brought from
a mountain named Lebanon; the Assyrians brought it to Babylon,
and from Babylon the Carians and Ionians brought it to Susa."

The subjects themselves might have had somewhat different
views of their purpose in life. Most subject peoples remained loyal
to the Persian empire, though the Egyptians rebelled again and
again; but across the vast realm there were many patterns of living.
The historian Herodotus tells the story that once Darius called before him some Greeks and asked how much he must pay them to eat
the bodies of their fathers when they died. The Greeks said in horror that nothing could bribe them to do so. Then Darius brought

in some Indians, of a tribe which did eat their fathers, and inquired through an interpreter how much he must give them to burn their fathers' bodies (as the Greeks did). "They uttered a cry of horror and forbade him to mention such a dreadful thing."

So too the contributions of the subject peoples to human development were not necessarily those which Darius would have stressed. In fact the two peoples we would consider most memorable, the Phoenicians and the Hebrews, are famous for ideas and beliefs which the Persian kings probably would have considered of little or no importance.

The Phoenicians

The land of Phoenicia is a narrow strip between mountains and sea, about 200 miles in length and rarely over 20 miles in width. There are small plains which rise into terraced hills; along the seacoast were many towns in antiquity, the houses of which were close-packed buildings of several stories. The chief cities from south to north were Tyre, Sidon, Berytus (now Beirut, capital of Lebanon), Byblos, and Aradus. Byblos at least went back to the 3d millennium B.C.; all had been ruled by the pharaohs of the New Kingdom; and several centers had been destroyed by the great invasion of 1200 B.C. The Semitic-speaking stock of the area survived this blow, and the cities began to revive from about 1000 B.C. on. Tyre, located on an island just offshore, became the major state of Phoenicia, partly because a great king, Hiram (about 970-940), the friend of Solomon, developed its trade and improved the harbor.

Phoenician craftsmen developed an amalgam of earlier artistic ideas, often of Egyptian origin. This cosmopolitan style was expressed in works of bronze, ivory, wood, textiles (often dyed a Tyrian purple), and other media. Phoenician ivories have turned up in Nineveh in quantities; bronzes of Phoenicia have been found in Cyprus and Crete; gold and other precious work were buried in tombs of the Etruscan people north of Rome. These popular wares were peddled widely, especially by sea.

Before 800 B.C. the Phoenicians were trading in Cyprus. Not long after that date they plunged all the way west to northwestern Africa to gain slaves, metals, and wheat. They established posts at Utica, Carthage, and westward as far as Spain. To understand the full meaning of this Phoenician expansion overseas one would have

An Assyrian relief of a Phoenician galley in open sea. Its prow ends in a ram; above is a row of shields. The sculptor gave play to his imagination by depicting a crab which has caught a fish.

to go into Greek and Roman history as far as the time of the great Carthaginian opponent of Rome, Hannibal. At this point we can sum it up by saying that the Phoenicians were one of the earliest means by which Near Eastern civilization was spread along the shores of the Mediterranean.

The Alphabet

For us the important legacy of the Phoenicians is the alphabet. Already in the days of the Egyptian New Kingdom the inhabitants of one Phoenician city (Ugarit) had experimented in using a cuneiform script with 30 signs for single consonants (and 3 vowels). This was a true alphabet, but at the same time other Semitic-speaking peoples of the area were creating alphabets of a more cursive style, some of the letters of which were derived from hieroglyphic symbols.

Before 1000 B.C. there had appeared north Semitic and south Semitic alphabets. The latter, known from Arabian examples, eventually produced the Ethiopian alphabet; the former gave rise to the

Phoenician and very similar Aramaic alphabets. These used only 22 signs, each of which stood for a consonantal sound, and were written from right to left. The script was admirably suited for the setting down of all kinds of information, both economic and literary, and could be learned easily. The peoples who accepted it did not need to create the learned type of scribe which had been common in the earlier Near East.

The new style spread as trade revived in the Near East, and alphabets throughout the Mediterranean drew from the Phoenician form. Probably just after 800 B.C. the Greeks adopted this alphabet together with the names of its letters (alpha = aleph, beta = beth, gamma = gimel), but for their own purposes they changed the phonetic values of some letters to stand for vowels. Far off in the other direction the Indians settled on a form of writing which was derived from the Aramaic version of the alphabet.

Development of the Alphabet

Phoenician	Early Greek	Later Greek	Latin	English
𐤀	✶𐤀	Α	A	A
𐤁	𐤁 𐤁	Β	B	B
𐤂	𐤂𐤂	Γ	C G	C G
𐤃	△	△	D	D
𐤄	𐤄	Ε	E	E

Political History of the Hebrews ❋ ❋ ❋ ❋ ❋ ❋ ❋ ❋ ❋ ❋ ❋ ❋ ❋ ❋ ❋ ❋ ❋

Just south of the Phoenicians, in the hills which stretched from the Jordan valley westward to the coastal plain, lay the Hebrews. These people stood apart from Near Eastern ways in many important respects.

In earlier days the Hebrews had been semi-nomadic, organized in patriarchal tribes; but eventually they secured mastery over the hill country of Palestine, or Canaan as it was then called. Their greatest political power was in the 10th century B.C., after the Egyptian New Kingdom had fallen and before Assyria began to dominate the Near East. In later times men looked back to the glories of the reign of king Solomon (about 965-925).

True, subsequent generations could not entirely forget that the building of the temple at Jerusalem and Solomon's palace had been the fruits of royal autocracy. Even in his lifetime there was grumbling over the requirement that men work four months of every year on the king's buildings, and parts of his state broke away. On his death the Hebrews refused to endure the perpetuation of this conventional Near Eastern absolutism and split apart. The northern kingdom, which was called Israel, had its capital at Samaria; the smaller southern state, Judah, was centered about Jerusalem.

The political vicissitudes of Israel and Judah are retailed at great length in the Old Testament so as to show God's hand at work. This history is told in terms of the people as a whole, not of the kings alone. At the time the kings were a powerful element in the worship of God, but as later tradition looked back it witheringly condemned almost all the monarchs for slipping off into the worship of foreign gods and for mistreating their subjects, who are nonetheless presented as far from perfect. Politically, indeed, the small kingdoms of Palestine had an ever more hopeless position, for the course of development across the Near East was toward empire.

Israel fell to Assyria in 722 B.C.; Judah lingered, off in the hills, longer. Its temple at Jerusalem was destroyed by Nebuchadrezzar of Babylon in 586 B.C. Thereafter the Hebrews were independent only for a brief period in the 2d to 1st centuries B.C. until recent times. Politically the tale of the Hebrews was a somber one. Solely when the rest of the Near East was weak could they hope to be independent, but their very reluctance to permit autocracy may have made the collapse of their kingdoms more inevitable. Yet the trials which afflicted the Hebrews are directly connected with the purification of their belief in God as unique and as an ethical force.

Hebrew Religion ✿✿✿✿✿✿✿✿✿✿✿✿✿✿✿✿✿✿✿✿✿✿✿✿

Late in the 2d millennium B.C. the Hebrews had a great leader, Moses, and under his guidance a new covenant was made with God which bound Him and His worshippers by a far more definite and conscious set of rules and beliefs than had existed earlier. Thenceforth the Lord was named YHWH. Since vowels were not written at this time, we can only guess that this term was pronounced Yahweh (= Jehovah).

Once Moses had made his covenant with God, the Hebrews and Yahweh were closely bound together. Always the Hebrews faced the temptation to drift into the worship of alien gods of more developed character and cult, first the agricultural deities of Canaan, then the imperial divinities of the Assyrian overlords. Time after time the chosen people of Yahweh slid away into foreign abomination; yet the basic spirit of reverence for Yahweh never quite yielded.

While the covenant was thus an enduring force in Hebrew history, one may doubt if the Hebrews would have continued their allegiance had they not steadily developed their concept of Yahweh. The unfolding of Hebrew religious thought is the principal underlying theme of the Old Testament; and certainly the Hebrews had a long road to travel in shaping their conception of God.

At the outset the existence of other gods was admitted. "Who," says Exodus 15:11, "is like unto Thee, O Lord, among the gods?" But Yahweh was a "jealous" god whom His chosen people must alone worship; from this root came slowly the claim of monotheism.

Nor was Yahweh initially described or defined in primarily ethical terms. He was a god of storms who appeared now in the cloud, now in a burning bush. His voice was the thunder, His arrow the lightning, and He was above all "a man of war." It may even have been believed that He usually lived in a box borne along with the Hebrews upon a wagon, the Ark of the Covenant, but He was not incarnated in a physical statue. His worship revolved about the bloody sacrifice of beasts, parts of whose carcasses were burned while the rest was cooked and eaten by the celebrants. With the feast inevitably went the consumption of much wine, and a veritable din must have risen on high beside the spiraling smoke of the altar. If we could suddenly see David "leaping and dancing before the Lord" (II Samuel 6:16) we might feel that we had stumbled on some aboriginal rite. The "righteous" conduct which Yahweh demanded from His adherents thus far meant little more than proper celebration of the ritual.

In the maintenance of ancestral beliefs and in the evolution of new concepts a large part was played by the priests of the temples of Yahweh. On one side they elaborated the worship of their God as an agricultural divinity—many of the enduring festivals of Judaism (Passover in the spring, Rosh Hashana in the fall) have close connections with the farming year—and they borrowed many aspects of the developed worship of the Canaanite *baals*. Yet on the other hand they maintained the uniqueness of Yahweh and fought against the tendency of the king to seize control of the religious machinery. Another potent force was the remarkable surge of lay readers from the people itself, the famous prophets.

Voice of the Prophets

The ancient Near East had long known foretellers of the future, who interpreted dreams, examined the livers of sheep, watched the flight of birds, or observed the stars. Generally such men were professionals and were organized in guilds, which handed down the secrets from father to son; commonly they worked primarily for the kings. The prophets of the Hebrews were of quite a different sort. They were called out of the people by an imperious inner drive to speak the words of God; they addressed commoners as well as monarchs; and their prophecies were far more criticisms of the present than predictions of coming events.

Sometimes these prophets spoke almost from frenzy in an ecstatic, involved style full of veiled meanings. At times too the prophets engaged in symbolic acts, as when Jeremiah broke a pot at the gate of Jerusalem to suggest its coming doom. But other figures, like Isaiah and Amos, were relatively straightforward in their sober, calculating, yet fiery judgment.

Whatever their approach, the theme of virtually all the prophets was the same. The covenant linked for all time God and His chosen people, who would be protected if they freely rendered Him the proper service. The alternative, which was expressed at times in prediction of the future, was grim: if the Hebrews went astray in the worship of foreign gods or in unrighteous behavior, Yahweh would punish them the more severely.

The prophets stood beside the priests in making religion the dominant thread of life, in attacking the wiles of foreign religions, and in calling for a return to earlier ways. Far more than the priests, however, the prophets described a righteous life in ethical terms. When the prophets saw the king or the rich oppressing the poor, reveling in luxury while the humble were sold into slavery, marrying foreign wives who brought alien social and religious customs, they cried out in rebuke, whatever the cost to themselves in scorn or even physical punishment. As the priesthood slowly codified ancestral customs in the law of Moses, its activity was strongly affected by the prophetic insistence that purity lay more in the attitude of the heart than in ritual observance. The burden of living by God's law was ever more clearly placed on the conscience of each individual follower of Yahweh.

In their message the prophets were rarely pleasant to hear and not always easy to fathom; yet in the course of Hebrew history their voice was both commanding and consoling. Perhaps such minor peoples as the Hebrews were bound to suffer at the hands of the Assyrians and the Babylonians, but the prophets helped their people to understand this oppression as the result of God's will. Always in the background lay the prophetic promise that if Israel purged itself it would be forgiven. In ethical matters the prophets were radical, but in terms of social and economic organization they were conservative and did not insist on sweeping reforms.

From the 6th century B.C. on their words were written down. Although edited in later days, the prophetic view was incorporated into the main body of Biblical thinking. Across later ages the Hebrew prophets have appealed to many generations as a tremendous outcry against man's injustice to man and as a chant of God's mercy.

The Uniqueness of Judaism ❋❋❋❋❋❋❋❋❋❋❋❋❋❋❋❋❋❋❋❋

Religiously the Hebrews—or as they have been called in more recent times, the Jews—had rejected the dross of paganism, including polytheism, the worship of gods in human form who were represented in statues and symbols, magic, and that mumbo-jumbo of fertility cults which often led to ritual murder and prostitution. Judaism stood alone in its emphasis on the uniqueness of God, to be worshipped by righteous men.

> It has been shown to you, O man, what is good
> and what the Lord requires of you:
> Only to do justice
> and to love loyally
> and to walk humbly with your God.

This was not an easy faith. It appealed to the individual and gave him a new freedom; yet it thereby placed upon him an added responsibility for his deeds and fenced him in with many rigid rules. Judaism was not mystical. It was a religion for men who lived in this world, but those who accepted it realized that physical temptations and material matters were secondary. In the trials of life, however, they might pray to a just God, one of Whose greatest marks was divine forgiveness. Not the least among the achievements of this faith, when one considers the character of Western civilization, was the insistence of the prophets that God dealt with each man by himself and their rejection of absolute kingship when God called one to stand for justice. Nowhere in the ancient Near East does there occur such a magnificent gallery of individual human figures as in the pages of the Old Testament.

In its account of the origin of the world and in many other respects this great book of Judaism passed on to the Western world some important parts of ancient Near Eastern thought. Judaism did not rise entirely apart from the Near East, and at times its followers were tempted back into magic and other older ideas. Yet it was far enough off the mainstream not to be greatly popular within the Near Eastern world. The higher ethical and spiritual beliefs incorporated in Judaism and its promise of a close relationship between the individual human being and the divine were not widely known in the Mediterranean world until the last century B.C. and later. The words of the prophets then were a powerful influence in Christianity and Islam alike, as well as in their own right in the continuing existence of Judaism.

A Look Back

In considering the Phoenicians and Hebrews we have been looking at Near Eastern peoples who directly affected the ways in which we write and think today in the Western world; but then too, many of the ideas inherent in Persian monarchy have had a great influence on modern European monarchies. From the past comes the inheritance of the present, even though each of us may use and outwardly alter that inheritance in many different ways.

Years B.C.	Empires	Palestine
1000		David
		Solomon
900	Revival of arts and trade	Division of kingdom
	Assyrian Empire	
750	Tiglath-Pileser III	Amos
		Isaiah
		Fall of Israel
700		
650		
612	Fall of Nineveh	Jeremiah
	Median and Babylonian Empires	
	Nebuchadrezzar	Fall of Judah
		Second Isaiah
550	**Persian Empire**	
	Cyrus	
	Cambyses	
500	Darius	

Men, after all, still died as a rule before they were 40, and during their brief lifetimes were subject to many internal worries and outside demands. Most men and women were desperately poor and often may not have eaten as much as their bodies needed; pestilence and infant diseases were terrific slayers. Are these, however, the aspects which the historian should stress as the conclusion of his tale? In Egypt the pyramids still stand today as "an act of faith"; the books which Christians call the Old Testament have been an enduring source of comfort and inspiration for common folk and artists. The ultimate question for every reader is whether the developments we have looked at are simply change or real progress, and the answer which each person will give about the meaning of the past will depend primarily upon his views of the future.

The pages of this book have described briefly perhaps a million years of human history. During almost all this tremendously long period men scavenged and gathered their food, but in the relatively brief period after about 8/7000 B.C. they learned first how to cultivate plants and domesticate animals and then to group themselves within the bonds of civilized order. Man's control over nature went hand in hand with his control over himself. By 500 B.C. life had become complex and intricate, and not all the results of civilization could be called blessings.

Art of Empire

Gold drinking vessel of the Persian period.

ARTS OF EMPIRE

The greatness of the Assyrians is perhaps most evident in the mammoth palaces they built at Nineveh and other sites; the huge mounds which still contain their remains have been excavated for over a century and yet have many secrets to be discovered. The Assyrian kings also built temples to Ashur, Ishtar, and the other gods and goddesses who protected their lands and peoples, but these temples were often virtually parts of the palaces.

In their artistic aspects and building techniques the palaces reflect an inheritance from Babylonian, Syrian, and other sources. At each corner an inscription in clay or precious metal was buried to ensure divine protection. The exterior was heavily walled; inside was a maze of servants' quarters, harem area, treasuries, and state apartments. Great audience halls, which were a focus for public activities, were built in rectangular shape with a throne platform against one long side and sometimes with an arched roof.

In the minor palaces the corridors and major rooms were adorned with painted frescoes, as had been the custom in the 2d millennium B.C., but for the great palaces veritable miles of stone relief were carved on gypsum slabs about seven feet high. These surfaces, which gave room either for one large band or more often two smaller bands of relief, admit us to the fascinating world of Assyrian monarchy.

Everywhere the king stands as the center of attention; the divine realm is suggested at times by winged and other gods or by the winged sun-disk in which Ashur rides above the head of his earthly representative. Sometimes the king dines in lovely gardens planted with trees and fruits; elsewhere tribute bearers bring him the riches of the empire; in the hunt scenes he unerringly draws his bow from his great chariot; often he leads his troops in war. While the slow-moving chronicle of inevitable victory is monotonous, it is also impressive.

From the artistic point of view Assyrian relief was the highest point thus far reached in Near Eastern art. Sieges and battles at times had almost a sense of space, and in the scenes of hunting the animals were shown with more realism than had ever before been achieved. Here the artists gave a vivid sense of motion, even at times of pity for the dying lions or wild asses. In other scenes the king, with fringed robe, long, curled beard, and heavy shoulders and legs, was a static but powerful figure.

Beside this great relief work in stone the Assyrian palaces at times were decorated with colorful scenes in baked tiles, and the gates were guarded by huge human-headed bulls or lions. Free-standing sculpture was scanty, but the rooms of the palaces must have blazed in their prime with products of the minor arts. Modern excavators have found scraps of glass and of the ivory work, in Phoenician, Syrian, and other

The bands of relief which decorated the great Assyrian palaces are varied in their scenes. The figure of a dying lioness to the left (facing page) catches the spirit of ultimate defiance; the attack on a fortress is more historical in character. The defenders resist, but many are already falling from the walls or floating dead in the river. Other Assyrian reliefs are shown on pp. 150 and 162.

styles, which adorned the beds and chairs; most of the gold and silver vessels, looted or made at royal command, have long since been melted down.

In Assyrian times the artistic traditions of the Near East were drawn together in an imperial style which remained the model through the days of king Nebuchadrezzar at Babylon into Persian times. The ability of Persian metal workers can be seen in surviving gold and silver drinking cups and ornaments, which are beautifully polished in their details and harmonious in appearance; Persian sculpture is best appreciated in the reliefs at the secluded royal fortress and treasury of Persepolis.

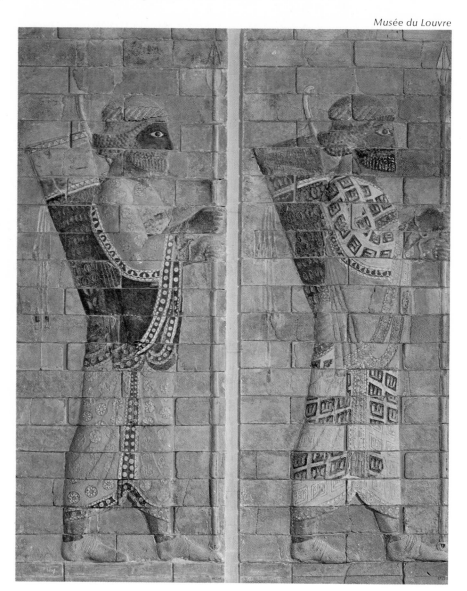

A Persian guard at Susa. The technique is directly derived from the Babylonian examples in the previous pictures.

In the 6th century B.C. the great street of Babylon used for the New Year's procession was decorated with a gate and walls covered by baked clay bricks. These show rows of bulls (a symbol of life) and of an imaginary creature called a "mushhush" (a symbol of the underworld).

Here, on a majestic site over a mile high, Darius built a great terrace from 512 B.C. on. This platform he and his successors adorned with huge gateways, staircases, palaces, colonnaded audience halls, and other buildings. The whole structure was about twice the size of the Acropolis at Athens, and the contrast between Persepolis and the sacred hill of the Greek goddess Athena illuminates sharply some fundamental differences between Greeks and Persians. While the Parthenon and other temples of the Acropolis were erected in honor of the patron deities of a free citizenry, the complex of Persepolis celebrated the greatness of the king of kings. His titles appeared on the window sills; he himself was depicted on his throne on the doorjambs, supported by figures representing the satrapies; the two staircases leading up to the great audience hall (which could hold 10,000 people) were decorated with reliefs showing the New Year's festival at the spring equinox, as illustrated on pp. 154 and 156.

The art of Persepolis is, at first sight, impressive in its pomp; but beside the graceful, dynamic, humane feeling imparted by the Greek

Lion biting a bull, from the staircase at Persepolis illustrated on p. 154. This motif has been used for many centuries in the Near East, and was borrowed by Greek artists later. Few examples, however, can match this one in its artistic balance and perfection of detail.

Oriental Institute, University of Chicago

reliefs of the Parthenon the spirit of the Persian work is solemn, static, and purely decorative. On the Persepolis reliefs, true, there is a rich diversity of local costumes, reflecting the great variety of the Near Eastern peoples, whereas the Athenian men and women of the Parthenon frieze are externally alike; yet the Greek figures are moved by a spiritual force which is totally absent in the Persian parades (and no women are shown at Persepolis).

Persian art is a fitting conclusion to our story, for it illustrates clearly how great a change was to come when the Greeks developed their civilization. Yet the work of Persian craftsmen in stone and metal must attract a man of the modern world far more than do the artistic products of early Mesopotamia 2000 years earlier. During those millennia the Near East had changed tremendously—but in an essentially continuous line of development. King Darius of Persia bore titles which had been coined by the world's first great imperialist, Sargon of Agade; the artists who worked in Persia used techniques and symbols which were equally ancient.

Man-headed bull capital from Persepolis.

SOURCES ON PERSIAN TIMES

A. DARIUS SEIZES THE THRONE

Students of modern history can read many sources, though an abundance of evidence does not mean that they can always establish exactly what happened or explain why it occurred. In ancient history, on the other hand, it is very rare to have two major accounts of the same event. During the period covered in this book there is only one good example—the rise of Darius to be king of the Persian empire after he had killed an usurper.

One account is Darius' own story, which he had carved on a rock cliff at Bisutun; the other is told by the Greek Herodotus, the Father of History. Herodotus lived from about 485 till after 430 B.C. and traveled through a good deal of the Persian empire.

Selections from these two accounts are given below. In re-creating the history of the past from its sources the historian must ask himself many questions. In this case, do the stories agree entirely? If not, why? Is Darius trying to prove anything in particular about his right to rule? Darius was a devout Zoroastrian and believed in the Truth; yet can we trust his official document? As for Herodotus, did he have any reason not to be impartial? How could he have known about the events? Does he make Darius solely responsible for the overthrow of Gaumata?

1. The Account of Darius

I am Darius the Great King, King of Kings, King in Persia, King of countries, son of Hystaspes, grandson of Arsames, an Achaemenian.

Says Darius the King: VIII of our family there are who were kings before; I am the ninth; IX in succession we have been kings.

Says Darius the King: By the favor of Ahuramazda I am King; Ahuramazda bestowed the kingdom upon me.

Says Darius the King: These are the countries which came to me; by the favor of Ahuramazda I was king of them: Persia, Elam, Babylonia, Egypt, those who are beside the sea, Sardis, Ionia, Media, Armenia, Cappadocia, Parthia, Drangiana, Aria, Chorasmia, Bactria, Sogdiana, Gandara, Scythia, Sattagydia, Arachosia, Maka: in all, XXII provinces.

Says Darius the King: Within these countries, the man who was loyal, him I rewarded well; him who was evil, him I punished well; by the favor of Ahuramazda these countries showed respect toward my law; as was said to them by me, thus was it done.

Says Darius the King: This is what was done by me after I became king. A son of Cyrus, Cambyses by name, of our family—he was king here. Of that Cambyses there was a brother, Smerdis by name. Afterwards, Cambyses slew that Smerdis. When Cambyses slew Smerdis, it did not become known to the people that Smerdis had been slain. Afterwards, Cambyses went to Egypt. When Cambyses had gone off to Egypt, after that the people became evil. After that the Lie waxed great in the country, both in Persia and in Media and in the other provinces.

Says Darius the King: Afterwards, there was one man, a Magian, Gaumata by name. He lied to the people thus: "I am Smerdis, the son of Cyrus, brother of Cambyses." After that, all the people became rebellious from Cambyses, and went over to him, both Persia and Media and the other provinces. He seized the kingdom; of the month Garmapada IX days were past, then he seized the kingdom. After that, Cambyses died by his own hand.

Says Darius the King: There was not a man, neither a Persian nor a Mede nor anyone of our family, who might make that Gaumata the Magian deprived of the kingdom. The people feared him greatly, thinking that he would slay in numbers the people who previously had known Smerdis. Not anyone dared say anything about Gaumata the Magian, until I came. After that I besought help of Ahuramazda; Ahuramazda bore me aid; of the month Bagayadi X days were past, then I with a few men slew that Gaumata the Magian, and those who were his foremost followers. A fortress by name Sikayauvati, a district by name Nisaya, in Media—there I slew him. I took the kingdom from him. By the favor of Ahuramazda I became king; Ahuramazda bestowed the kingdom on me.

Above is the great inscription of Darius at Bisutun. The white area is covered with latex rubber to make a "squeeze" or copy which can be studied at leisure. Just to its right is the winged sun disk of Ahura Mazda.

Below is the head of Darius. Apparently the beard was not successfully carved from the native stone; it is a separate block which has been pegged into the cliff by iron bars (the holes for the pegs can be seen in the neck of Darius and to the right of his mouth).

George G. Cameron

Says Darius the King: The kingdom which had been taken away from our family, that I put in its place; I reestablished it on its foundation. As before, so I made the sanctuaries which Gaumata the Magian destroyed. I restored to the people the pastures and the herds, the household slaves and the houses which Gaumata the Magian took away from them. I reestablished the people on its foundation, both Persia and Media and the other provinces. As before, so I brought back what had been taken away. By the favor of Ahuramazda this I did: I strove until I reestablished our royal house on its foundations as it was before. So I strove, by the favor of Ahuramazda, so that Gaumata the Magian did not remove our royal house.

After recounting other victories, Darius sums up the reasons for his victories:

Says Darius the King: You who shall be king hereafter, protect yourself vigorously from the Lie; the man who shall be a Lie–follower, punish him well if you shall think thus, "May my country be secure!"

Says Darius the King: This is what I did; by the favor of Ahuramazda, in one and the same year I did it. You who shall hereafter read this inscription, let what which has been done by me convince you; do not think it a lie.

Says Darius the King: For this reason Ahuramazda bore aid, and the other gods who are, because I was not hostile, I was not a Lie-follower, I was not a doer of wrong—neither I nor my family. According to righteousness I conducted myself. Neither to the weak nor to the powerful did I do wrong. The man who cooperated with my house, him I rewarded well; whoso did injure, him I punished well.

Says Darius the King: These are the men who were there at the time when I slew Gaumata the Magian who called himself Smerdis; at that time these men cooperated as my followers: Intaphernes, Otanes, Gobryas, Hydarnes, Megabyzus, Ardumanish.

Says Darius the King: You who shall be king hereafter, protect well the family of these men.

Says Darius the King: By the favor of Ahuramazda this is the inscription which I made. Besides, it was in Aryan, and on clay tablets and on parchment it was composed. Besides, a sculptured figure of myself I made. Besides, I made my lineage. And it was inscribed and read off before me. Afterwards this inscription I sent off everywhere among the provinces.* The people unitedly worked upon it.

* This translation is from the Old Persian (=Aryan) version at Bisutun. There survive parts of an Akkadian version from Babylon and of an Aramaic version on papyrus, found at Elephantine in southern Egypt.

2. Herodotus' Account

Herodotus also tells us Cambyses killed his brother. He adds further statements that Cambyses killed his sister (whom he had married) after conquering Egypt and that from birth Cambyses suffered from epilepsy. In Egypt he was reported to have mocked the local religion and killed the sacred bull Apis.

Cambyses, son of Cyrus, after going out of his mind, still lingered on in Egypt; and while he was there, two brothers, who belonged to the caste of the Magi, rose in rebellion against him at home. One of them—Patizeithes—had been left by Cambyses as controller of his household during his absence, and this was the one who planned the revolt. Aware that Smerdis was dead, but that his death was concealed from all but a few of the Persians, most of whom believed that he was still alive, he took advantage of this state of affairs to make a bold bid for the throne. The brother, whom I have already mentioned as his confederate, bore a close resemblance to Cyrus' son Smerdis, Cambyses' murdered brother. Beside the physical likeness, it also happened that he bore the same name. Patizeithes having persuaded this brother of his that he would successfully carry the business through, made him take his seat upon the royal throne, and then sent out a proclamation to the troops, not only throughout Persia but also in Egypt, that they should take their orders in future not from Cambyses but from Smerdis.

[On receiving this news] Cambyses leapt upon his horse, meaning to march with all speed to Susa and attack the Magus. But as he was springing into the saddle, the cap fell off the sheath of his sword, exposing the blade, which pierced his thigh.

[After telling the chief Persians with the army that Smerdis really was dead, Cambyses himself died; but the empire accepted the Magus for a while.] During this time his subjects received great benefits from him, and he was regretted after his death by all the Asiatics under his rule, though not by the Persians themselves. To every nation within his dominion he proclaimed, directly he came to the throne, a three years' remission of taxes and military service. But after seven months of power, the following circumstances led to his exposure. The first person to suspect that he was not the son of Cyrus but an imposter, was a certain Otanes, the son of Pharnaspes, one of the wealthiest members of the Persian nobility, and his suspicions were aroused by the fact that Smerdis never ventured outside the central fortifications of the capital, and never summoned any eminent Persian to a private audience.

[Otanes had his daughter, who was in the harem of the king, feel the ears of the imposter at night; for the Magus had had his ears cut off during the reign of Cyrus for a crime. She found he had no ears and managed to get word of the fact to her father.] Otanes took into his confidence Aspathines and Gobryas, two eminent Persians whom he had special reason to trust, and told them of his discovery. Both these men already had their suspicions of the truth, and were ready enough, in consequence, to accept what Otanes said, and it was then agreed that each of the three should choose his most trustworthy friend and bring him in as an accomplice. Otanes chose Intaphrenes, Gobryas Megabyzus, and Aspathines Hydarnes. The number of conspirators was thus raised to six, and on the arrival at Susa from Persia of Darius, whose father Hystaspes was governor there, it was decided to add him to the number.

[After making their plans, they went to the palace.] The sentries, out of respect for their exalted rank, and having no suspicion of the real purpose of their visit, allowed them to pass without question— almost as if they were under the special protection of heaven. In the great court, however, they were met by some of the eunuchs—the king's messengers—who stopped them and asked their business, at the same time threatening the guards for having let them through. The check was momentary; eager to pass on, the seven, with a word of mutual encouragement, drew their daggers, stabbed the eunuchs who were trying to hold them up, and ran forward into the hall.

Both the Magi were at this time indoors. They heard the eunuchs crying out in evident alarm, and sprang up to see what the matter was; then, realizing their danger, they at once prepared to fight it out. One just had time to get his bow down, the other made do with his spear—and the struggle began. The one with the bow had no chance to use it—the fight was at much too close quarters; the other, however, used his spear to advantage, keeping off his attackers and wounding Aspathines in the leg, and Intaphrenes in the eye—Intaphrenes, as a result of the wound, lost his eye but survived. His companion, unable to use his bow and finding himself defenceless, ran into a bedroom, which opened out of the hall, and tried to shut the doors on his pursuers; but two of them, Darius and Gobryas, managed to force their way in with him, and Gobryas got his arms round the Magus. It was dark in the room, and Darius, standing over the two men locked together on the floor, hesitated to intervene; for he was afraid that, if he struck, he might kill the wrong man. But Gobryas, aware of his hesitation, cried out: "What's your hand for—if you don't use it?"

"I dare not strike," said Darius, "for fear of killing you."

"Fear nothing," answered Gobryas; "spit both of us at once—if need be."

Darius then drove his dagger home—by good luck into the body of the Magus.

B. THE HEBREW PROPHETS

The 24 books of the Old Testament were written, and sometimes rewritten, down to the last centuries B.C. For no other people of the Near East do we have such a remarkable collection of legal codes, moral rules, traditional poetry, mythological explanations, formal history, and commentary by great teachers and prophets.

To suggest the remarkable character of Hebrew moral and religious teachings we can look at part of the work of two great prophets. The first is the sheepmaster of Judah, Amos, who burst down on the northern kingdom of Israel about 750 B.C. and spoke of the forthcoming vengeance of God. His words are the first direct account of a prophet which survive in the Old Testament.

Beside him may be placed, for comparative purposes, the unknown prophet called the Second Isaiah, whose message to the captives in Babylonia (597-539 B.C.) was incorporated in the Book of Isaiah as Chapters 40 through 55.

Are there historical reasons why Amos was bitter and brief, the Second Isaiah ecstatic and optimistic? Can you detect any development between the two (about 2 centuries apart) in concepts of God as an unique, ethical figure? Incidentally the idea of the Second Isaiah that the Jews were a "suffering servant" for the benefit of all mankind was not one which later Judaism altogether accepted; but Christians took it as a prefiguration of Christ.

1. The Prophet Amos

Hear this word, you cows of Bashan,*
    who are in the mountain of Samaria,
who oppress the poor, who crush the needy,
    who say to their husbands, "Bring, that we may drink!"
The Lord God has sworn by his holiness
    that, behold, the days are coming upon you,
when they shall take you away with hooks,
    even the last of you with fishhooks.
And you shall go out through the breaches,
    every one straight before her;
and you shall be cast forth into Harmon,
                    says the Lord.

Come to Bethel, and transgress;
    to Gilgal, and multiply transgression;

* A satirical description of the ladies at the Israelite court.

bring your sacrifices every morning,
     your tithes every three days;
offer a sacrifice of thanksgiving of that which is leavened,
     and proclaim freewill offerings, publish them;
     for so you love to do, O people of Israel!
                        says the Lord God.

I gave you cleanness of teeth in all your cities,
     and lack of bread in all your places,
yet you did not return to me,
                        says the Lord.

And I also withheld the rain from you
     when there were yet three months to the harvest;
I would send rain upon one city,
     and send no rain upon another city;
one field would be rained upon,
     and the field on which it did not rain withered;
so two or three cities wandered to one city
     to drink water, and were not satisfied;
yet you did not return to me,
                        says the Lord.

I smote you with blight and mildew;
     I laid waste your gardens and your vineyards;
     your fig trees and your olive trees the locust devoured;
yet you did not return to me,
                        says the Lord.

I sent among you a pestilence after the manner of Egypt;
     I slew your young men with the sword;
I carried away your horses;
     and I made the stench of your camp go up into your nostrils;
yet you did not return to me,
                        says the Lord.

I overthrew some of you,
     as when God overthrew Sodom and Gomorrah,
     and you were as a brand plucked out of the burning;
yet you did not return to me,
                        says the Lord.

Therefore thus I will do to you, O Israel;
     because I will do this to you.
     prepare to meet your God, O Israel!

For lo, he who forms the mountains, and creates the wind,
     and declares to man what is his thought;

who makes the morning darkness,
    and treads on the heights of the earth—
the Lord, the God of hosts, is his name!

Therefore thus says the Lord, the God of hosts, the Lord:
In all the squares there shall be wailing;
    and in all the streets they shall say, "Alas! alas!"
They shall call the farmers to mourning
    and to wailing those who are skilled in lamentation,
and in all vineyards there shall be wailing,
    for I will pass through the midst of you,
                says the Lord.

Woe to you who desire the day of the Lord!
    Why would you have the day of the Lord?
It is darkness, and not light; as if a man fled from a lion, and
        a bear met him;
    or went into the house and leaned with his hand against the wall,
    and a serpent bit him.
Is not the day of the Lord darkness, and not light,
    and gloom with no brightness in it?

I hate, I despise your feasts,
    and I take no delight in your solemn assemblies.
Even though you offer me your burnt offerings and cereal offerings,
    I will not accept them,
and the peace offerings of your fatted beasts
    I will not look upon.
Take away from me the noise of your songs;
    to the melody of your harps I will not listen.
But let justice roll down like waters,
    and righteousness like an ever-flowing stream.

2. The Second Isaiah
    Comfort, comfort my people,
        says your God.
    Speak tenderly to Jerusalem,
        and cry to her
    that her warfare is ended
        that her iniquity is pardoned,
    that she has received from the Lord's hand
        double for all her sins.

    A voice cries:
    "In the wilderness prepare the way of the Lord,
        Make straight in the desert a highway for our God.

Every valley shall be lifted up,
    and every mountain and hill be made low;
the uneven ground shall become level,
    and the rough places a plain.
And the glory of the Lord shall be revealed,
    and all flesh shall see it together,
    for the mouth of the Lord has spoken."

A voice says, "Cry!"
    And I said, "What shall I cry?"
All flesh is grass,
    and all its beauty is like the flower of the field.
The grass withers, the flower fades;
    when the breath of the Lord blows upon it,
    surely the people is grass.
The grass withers, the flower fades;
    but the word of our God will stand for ever.

. . .

Remember these things, O Jacob,
    and Israel, for you are my servant;
I formed you, you are my servant;
    O Israel, you will not be forgotten by me.
I have swept away your transgressions like a cloud,
    and your sins like mist;
return to me, for I have redeemed you.

Sing, O heavens, for the Lord has done it;
    shout, O depths of the earth;
break forth into singing, O mountains,
    O forest, and every tree in it!
For the Lord has redeemed Jacob,
    and will be glorified in Israel.

Thus says the Lord, your Redeemer,
    who formed you from the womb:
"I am the Lord, who made all things,
    who stretched out the heavens alone,
    who spread out the earth—Who was with me?—
who frustrates the omens of liars,
    and makes fools of diviners;
who turns wise men back,
    and makes their knowledge foolish;
who confirms the word of his servant,
    and performs the counsel of his messengers;
who says of Jerusalem, 'She shall be inhabited,'

and of the cities of Judah, 'They shall be built,
    and I will raise up their ruins';
who says to the deep, 'Be dry,
    and I will dry up your rivers';
who says of Cyrus, 'He is my shepherd,
    and he shall fulfil all my purpose';
saying of Jerusalem, 'She shall be built,'
    and of the temple, 'Your foundation shall be laid.'"

Thus says the Lord to his anointed, To Cyrus,
    whose right hand I have grasped,
to subdue nations before him
    and ungird the loins of kings,
to open doors before him
    that gates may not be closed:
"I will go before you
    and level the mountains,
I will break in pieces the doors of bronze
    and cut asunder the bars of iron,
I will give you the treasures of darkness
    and the hoards in secret places,
that you may know that it is I, the Lord,
    the God of Israel, who call you by your name.
For the sake of my servant Jacob,
    and Israel my chosen,
I call you by your name,
    I surname you, though you do not know me.
I am the Lord, and there is no other,
    besides me there is no God;
    I gird you, though you do not know me,
that men may know, from the rising of the sun
    and from the west, that there is none besides me;
    I am the Lord, and there is no other."

.   .   .

Come down and sit in the dust,
    O virgin daughter of Babylon;
sit on the ground without a throne,
    O daughter of the Chaldeans!
For you shall no more be called
    tender and delicate.
Take the millstones and grind meal,
    put off your veil,
strip off your robe, uncover your legs,
    pass through the rivers.
Your nakedness shall be uncovered,

and your shame shall be seen.
I will take vengeance,
    and I will spare no man.
Our Redeemer—the Lord of hosts is his name—
    is the Holy One of Israel.

Sit in silence, and go into darkness,
    O daughter of the Chaldeans;
for you shall no more be called
    the mistress of kingdoms.

.   .   .

Behold my servant, whom I uphold,
    my chosen, in whom my soul delights;
I have put my Spirit upon him,
    he will bring forth justice to the nations.
He will not cry or lift up his voice,
    or make it heard in the street;
a bruised reed he will not break,
    and a dimly burning wick he will not quench;
    he will faithfully bring forth justice.
He will not fail or be discouraged
    till he has established justice in the earth;
    and the coastlands wait for his law.

SOURCES OF QUOTATIONS

PAGES

18   Ralph S. Solecki, *Shanidar* (New York: Knopf, 1971), p. 61, quoting the Wigrams.

80   James B. Pritchard, editor, *Ancient Near Eastern Texts Relating to the Old Testament* (2d ed.; Princeton: Princeton University Press, 1955), and *The Ancient Near East: Supplementary Text and Pictures Relating to the Old Testament* (Princeton: Princeton University Press, 1969), p. 270 [hereafter cited *ANET*; see note at end of list]

82   *ANET*, p. 207
       ANET, p. 269

83   *ANET*, p. 175

84   *ANET*, p. 178

85   *ANET*, p. 594

86   *ANET*, p. 266
       H. W. F. Saggs, *The Greatness That Was Babylon* (Mentor MJ859), p. 234

91   *ANET*, p. 79

92   *ANET*, p. 60

94   *ANET*, p. 593
       ANET, p. 525

97   Herodotus, Book II, chap. 35

107   J. H. Breasted, *Ancient Records of Egypt*, II (Chicago: University of Chicago Press, 1906), p. 40

112   J. H. Breasted, *Cambridge Ancient History*, II (Cambridge: Cambridge University Press, 1926), p. 95

133-40   *ANET*, pp. 580 (Enheduanna), 383 (Ishtar), 647-648, 650 (Agade), 105 (Atrahasis), 595-596 (Shuruppak), 585 (Shulgi), 90ff. (epic of Gilgamesh), 629 (letter), 640 (Inanna), 170ff. (code of Hammurapi), 545 (adoption)

141   A. Leo Oppenheim, *The Interpretation of Dreams in the Ancient Near East, Transactions of the American Philosophical Society*, new series vol. 46, part 3 (1956), pp. 228, 258, 264, 265, 269, 271, 276 (by permission of the American Philosophical Society and the author)

151   *ANET*, p. 297

152   *ANET*, p. 276

153   Nahum 3:1, 7
      ANET, p. 315

155   E. F. Schmidt, *Persepolis*, I (Chicago: University of Chicago Press, 1953), pp. 65 and 63
      Herodotus, Book I, chap. 136

160   A. T. Olmstead, *History of the Persian Empire* (Phoenix P36), p. 168

161   Herodotus, Book III, chap. 38

167   Micah 6:8, translated by Harry M. Orlinsky, *Ancient Israel* (Ithaca: Cornell University Press, 1954), p. 151

182-84   R. G. Kent, *Old Persian Grammar Texts Lexicon*, American Oriental Society vol. 33 (2d ed., 1953), pp. 119-120, 132

185-86   Herodotus, Book III, chaps. 61-78, translated by A. de Selincourt (by permission of Penguin Books Ltd)

187-89   Amos 4, 5

189-92   Isaiah 40, 44-45, 47, 42 (both in the translation of the *Oxford Annotated Bible* [New York: Oxford University Press, 1962])

Translations from the magnificent collection of Near Eastern texts by J. B. Pritchard (*ANET*) are reprinted by permission of the Princeton University Press, to which I am much indebted.

FURTHER READING

Any study of early man which was written more than 10 years ago is likely to be out-of-date, so rapidly does our evidence grow; but its ideas may still be important. For the subjects discussed in this book I have selected a few works which are recent, accurate, and generally interesting. Technical descriptions of specific excavations or highly theoretical interpretations of early man are omitted. The books which will be understood most easily are marked with an asterisk, but anyone interested in a specific topic should try the others that deal with it. For paperback editions only the series and number are given.

Very current information will be found in such magazines as *Antiquity, Archaeology, National Geographic Magazine, Natural History,* and *Scientific American.* These journals have excellent articles for the general reader, which are well illustrated.

Prehistory Generally: V. Gordon Childe, *What Happened in History** (Penguin A108), has had a great effect on our views of the prehistoric stages of human development. F. Clark Howell and the editors of Life, *Early Man** (New York: Time, 1965), has good reconstruction drawings; Robert J. Braidwood, *Prehistoric Men** (7th ed.; New York: Scott, Foresman, 1967), is straightforward.

More detailed accounts can be found in William Howells, *Mankind in the Making* (rev. ed.; New York: Doubleday, 1967); Grahame Clark, *World Prehistory: An Outline* (2d ed.; Cambridge: Cambridge University Press, 1969); François Bordes, *The Old Stone Age* (New York: McGraw-Hill, 1968). A balanced exploration of a much argued subject is Richard A. Goldsby, *Race and Races** (New York: Macmillan, 1971).

For dating, see Willard F. Libby's own account, *Radiocarbon Dating** (2d ed.; Chicago: University of Chicago Press, 1955); K. W. Butzer, *Environment and Archaeology* (Chicago: Aldine, 1964), on the geological framework; F. E. Zeuner, *Dating the Past* (4th ed.; London: Methuen, 1958), which is technical but clear. David O. Woodbury, *When the Ice Came** (New York: Dodd, Mead, 1963), tries to give an answer to the question why the glaciers expanded.

Archeology is a popular subject, well presented by Robert J. Braidwood, *Archaeologists and What They Do** (New York: Franklin Watts, 1960). Glyn Daniel, *The Idea of Prehistory* (Penguin A650), describes the evolution of archeological research; J. S. Wiener, *The Piltdown Forgery* (London: Oxford University Press, 1955), shows how one famous skull was proven a fake.

Specific Sites: J. M. Coles and E. S. Higgs, *The Archaeology of Early Man* (London: Faber and Faber, 1969), is a survey area by area. Kitchen middens, Danish bog sacrifices, Stonehenge, and other European finds are described by Geoffrey Bibby, *The Testimony of the Spade** (New York: Knopf, 1968).

For places discussed in this book see Linda J. Braidwood, *Digging Beyond the Tigris** (New York: Schuman, 1953); K. M. Kenyon, *Digging Up Jericho* (New York: Praeger, 1957); James Mellaart, *Çatal Hüyük* (New York: McGraw-Hill, 1967); Mina W. Mulvey, *Digging Up Adam** (New York: McKay, 1969), on Leakey's career; Ralph S. Solecki, *Shanidar** (New York: Knopf, 1971).

Prehistoric Life: The making of stone tools is explained by K. P. Oakley, *Man the Tool-Maker** (Phoenix P20) and amusingly by H. Mewhinney, *A Manual for Neanderthals** (Austin: University of Texas Press, 1957). How these tools were used to support life is discussed by J. G. D. Clark, *Prehistoric Europe: The Economic Basis* (London: Methuen, 1952), or more simply by I. W. Cornwall, *The World of Ancient Man** (New York: John Day, 1964), and *Prehistoric Animals and Their Hunters** (London: Faber and Faber, 1968).

Sensible essays on various aspects of prehistoric life are collected by Harry L. Shapiro, *Man, Culture, and Society* (Oxford Galaxy 32) or more recently by Sherwood L. Washburn, *Social Life of Early Man* (Chicago: Aldine, 1961). Both have bibliographies. On language see also Gega Révész, *The Origins and Prehistory of Language* (London: Longmans Green, 1956).

Hans-Georg Bandi and others, *The Art of the Stone Age* (New York: Crown, 1961), is a survey of cave art; one famous site is pictured in Georges Bataille, *Lascaux* (New York: Skira, 1955). Peter J. Ucko and Andrée Rosenfeld, *Paleolithic Cave Art* (New York: McGraw-Hill, 1967), is sensible on its interpretation.

Agriculture and Technology: Stuart Struever, ed., *Prehistoric Agriculture* (New York: American Museum of Natural History, 1971), has among other things an essay by R. S. MacNeish on Tehuacan. See also Don and Patricia Bothwell, *Food in Antiquity** (New York: Praeger, 1969); Sonia Cole, *The Neolithic Revolution** (3d ed.; London: British Museum, 1967); C. O. Sauer, *Agricultural Origins and Dispersals** (2d ed.; Cambridge, Mass.: MIT Press, 1969).

Henry Hodges, *Technology in the Ancient World** (New York: Knopf, 1970), is clear; the discovery of metals is outlined in R. J. Forbes, *Metallurgy in Antiquity* (Leiden: Brill, 1950). Other developments can be found in H. E. Sigerist, *History of Medicine*, vol. I (New York: Oxford University Press, 1951); Edwin Tunis, *Wheels** (Cleveland: World, 1955); Lionel Casson, *The Ancient Mariners** (Minerva M17).

Beginnings of Civilization: Important for their ideas, if somewhat out-dated factually, are Henri Frankfort, *Birth of Civilization in the Near East** (Anchor A89) and a work which he edited, *Before Philosophy* (Penguin A198). Robert J. Braidwood, *The Near East and the Foundations for Civilization* (Eugene: University of Oregon Press, 1952), is also thought-provoking. Stuart Piggott, ed., *The Dawn of Civilization* (London: Thames and Hudson, 1961), is a big picture book with essays. Robert McC. Adams, *The Evolution of Urban Society* (Chicago: Aldine, 1962), compares the origins of civilization in Mesopotamia and Mexico.

Mesopotamia: Archeological work is discussed by Seton Lloyd, *Foundations in the Dust* (Penguin A336). On the Sumerians see

S. N. Kramer, *History Begins at Sumer** (London: Thames and Hudson, 1958) and *The Sumerians** (Chicago: University of Chicago Press, 1958). H. W. F. Saggs, *The Greatness That Was Babylon* (Mentor MJ859) and *Everyday Life in Babylonia and Assyria* (New York: Putnam, 1965), are thorough.

Mesopotamian art is well interpreted by Henri Frankfort, *The Art and Architecture of the Ancient Orient* (Pelican PZ7). André Parrot, *Sumer: The Dawn of Art* (New York: Golden Press, 1961), and Anton Moortgat, *The Art of Ancient Mesopotamia* (London: Phaidon, 1969), give a good selection of pictures.

Egypt: The most illuminating work on Egyptian civilization is John A. Wilson, *Culture of Ancient Egypt* (Phoenix P11). Cyril Aldred, *The Egyptians* (Praeger P126), is briefer; Barbara Merz, *Red Land, Black Land** (New York: Coward-McCann, 1966), treats Egyptian life and death. There is a popular survey of the New Kingdom by Geoffrey Bibby, *Four Thousand Years Ago** (New York: Knopf, 1961), and of its daily life by Pierre Montet, *Everyday Life in Egypt* (New York: St. Martin's, 1958). J. H. Breasted, *Dawn of Conscience* (New York: Scribner, 1934), made popular the picture of Akhenaten as a great reformer; the tomb of Tutankhamen is described by C. Desroches-Noblecourt, *Tutankhamen* (Doubleday paperback).

On Egyptian art see I. Woldering, *Egypt* (London: Methuen, 1963), or more fully W. Stevenson Smith, *The Art and Architecture of Ancient Egypt* (Harmondsworth: Penguin, 1958); I. E. S. Edwards, *Pyramids of Egypt* (Penguin A168); Christine Price, *Made in Ancient Egypt** (New York: Dutton, 1970).

Near Eastern Empires: W. W. Hallo and W. K. Simpson, *The Ancient Near East* (Harcourt Brace Jovanovich, 143), give a brief summary which goes back to prehistoric times. A. T. Olmstead has written thorough but not very exciting books on *The History of Assyria* (New York: Scribner, 1923) and *History of the Persian Empire* (Phoenix P36). See also R. N. Frye, *Heritage of Persia* (Cleveland: World, 1963), and Donald N. Wilber, *Persepolis** (New York: Crowell, 1969).

The art of the empires is illustrated by André Parrot, *Arts of Assyria* (New York: Golden Press, 1961), and Edith Porada, *Ancient Iran* (London: Methuen, 1969). Other aspects are discussed by Georges Contenau, *Everyday Life in Babylonia and Assyria* (London: Arnold, 1951), and S. H. Hooke, *Babylonian and Assyrian Religion* (Norman: University of Oklahoma Press, 1963).

For other peoples of the Near East see O. S. Gurney, *The Hittites* (Penguin A259); S. Moscati, *Ancient Semitic Civilizations* (Capricorn 202); Donald Harden, *The Phoenicians* (Praeger P128). David Diringer, *Writing** (New York: Praeger, 1962), is clear.

The literature on the Hebrews and Judaism is immense. A few good works are Harry M. Orlinsky, *Ancient Israel** (Ithaca: Cornell University Press, 1954); Roland de Vaux, *Ancient Israel: Its Life and Institutions* (New York: McGraw-Hill, 1961); and on the Hebrew achievement as a whole Mary Ellen Chase, *Life and Language in the Old Testament* (Norton N109).

Stories and Biographies: For this early period it is difficult to write stories which have a solid base. You might like to try Erick Berry, *Honey of the Nile** (New York: Oxford University Press, 1938); Olivia Coolidge, *Egyptian Adventures** (Boston: Houghton Mifflin, 1954), short stories; William Golding, *The Inheritors* (Pocketbooks 75169), a symbolic tale in Neanderthal times; Harold Lamb, *Cyrus the Great** (New York: Doubleday, 1960), a biography.

The Epic of Gilgamesh is translated by N. K. Sanders (Penguin L100) and *Letters from Mesopotamia* by A. Leo Oppenheim (Chicago: University of Chicago Press, 1967). I have quoted several selections from J. B. Pritchard's *Ancient Near Eastern Texts;* but there is much more of interest in this work.

GLOSSARY

The following list provides brief identifications of major individuals and also definitions of unusual words in this book. As a guide to pronunciation I have marked, where necessary, the long vowels and the stressed syllables. All ancient dates are B.C., and most of these are not absolutely certain.

Achaemenes (ak-e-men'-ēz), founder of Persian royal dynasty
Adad (a'-dad), Mesopotamian weather god
Aegean Sea (ē-jē'-an), branch of Mediterranean Sea in which Greek culture was centered
Agade (a-gad'-e), capital of Sargon and Naram-Sin
Ahriman (a'-ri-man), evil deity in Zoroastrian belief
Ahura Mazda (a-hoo-ra-maz'-da), god of light and truth in Zoroastrian belief
Aketaten (ak'-e-ta-ten), capital of Egypt under Akhenaten
Akhenaten (ak'-e-nat-en), Egyptian religious reformer 1367-1350 [also spelled Ikhnaton]
Akitu (a-ki'-tu), Babylonian festival of New Year
Akkad (ak'-ad), middle Mesopotamia, occupied by Semitic-speaking peoples
Altamira (al-ta-mir'-a), cave in Spain where paintings of bulls were discovered in 1879
Amarna (a-mar'-na), modern name of Aketaten
Amen (a'-men), Egyptian sungod prominent in New Kingdom [also spelled Amon and Amun]
Amos, Hebrew prophet of 8th century
ankh (ank), Egyptian symbol of the "breath of life"
Annunaki (a-nun'-a-ki), assembly of Mesopotamian gods

anthropology, study of man, divided into physical anthropology (human physical development) and cultural anthropology (character and development of ways of life, both primitive and advanced)

antiquus (an-ti′-kwus), type of elephant in middle Pleistocene epoch; also type of extinct bison

Anu (a′-noō), Mesopotamian god of the sky

Anubis (a-noō′-bis), Egyptian jackal god who escorted dead to next world

Aramaic (ar-a-mā′-ik), Semitic language spoken in Syria and Persian empire

archeology, scientific study of material remains of human history, often but not always involving excavation

Ashur (a′-shoōr), capital of Assyria; also its main god

Assyria (a-sir′-ē-a), kingdom in upper Mesopotamia; empire to 612

Astarte (a-star′-tē), Semitic goddess of human fertility

Aten (a′-ten), Egyptian god of sun revered by Akhenaten

Atrahasis (a-tra-ha′-sis), Babylonian Noah

Australopithecine (o-strā-lō′pith-e-sīn), ancestor of man found in southern Africa

Babylon (bab′-e-lon), major city in Mesopotamia

Bel (bāl), Mesopotamian name for Marduk, "the lord" [also spelled Baal]

Berytus (be-rīt′-us), city in Phoenicia (now Beirut)

Bisutun (bē′-su-tun), cliff on which Darius carved record of his reign [also spelled Behistun]

Black, Davidson, 1884-1934, Canadian doctor who excavated in China

bola (bō′-la), cord with two or more balls attached to it, thrown to entangle animal

Boucher de Perthes, Jacques (bu-shā′ de pert′), 1788-1868, French archeologist who discovered flints together with extinct animals

Braidwood, Robert, b. 1907, excavator of Jarmo

burin (būr′-in), long thin chisel made by early *homo sapiens*

Byblos (bib′-los), city in Phoenicia

Cambyses (kam-bī′-sēz), Persian king 530-522, who conquered Egypt

Canaan (kā′-nen), early name for Palestine

Carmel, Mount, site in Israel where Neanderthal and Natufian remains have been found

cartouche (kar-toōsh′), oval containing Egyptian ruler's name

Çatal Hüyük (cha-tal hu′-yuk), early agricultural site in south-central Turkey

Cenozoic era (sē-nō-zō′-ik), most recent geological era, subdivided into Pleistocene and recent epochs

Choukoutien (jō′-kō-dyan), site of *homo erectus* southwest of Peking

civilization, stage of human development in which men lived in organized states

Croesus (krē′-sus), king of Lydia conquered by Cyrus in 547

Cro-Magnon (krō-mag′-non), French site at which early *homo sapiens* was found

culture, a way of living and making things which is passed on socially

cuneiform (kyu-nē'-i-form), Mesopotamian script using symbols of wedge shape

Cyrus (sī'-rus), founder of Persian empire, king 557-530

Darius (da-rī'-us), organizer of Persian imperial administration 521-486

Dart, Raymond, b. 1893, discoverer of Australopithecines

Deir el-Bahri (der-el-bah'-ri), funerary temple of queen Hatshepsut near Thebes

Delta, part of Egypt north of Cairo where the Nile divides into several streams

Dolní Věstonice (dol-ni' vyesh'-to-nit-se), site of *homo sapiens* in southern Czechoslovakia, 27-23,000 B.C.

Dubois, Eugène (dub-wa'), 1858-1941, Dutch discoverer of *homo erectus* in Java

Ea (ā'-a), Mesopotamian god of wisdom and waters

Ecbatana (ek-bat'-an-a), one of Persian capitals (now Hamadan)

einkorn (īn'-korn), primitive form of wheat cultivated mainly in Turkey in early times

emmer (em'-er), hard red wheat, more widely used than einkorn

Enheduanna (en-hā'-du-an-a), daughter of Sargon, priestess at Ur

Enkidu (en'-ki-du), friend of Gilgamesh

Enlil (en'-lil), Mesopotamian god of earth and wind

Esagil (ā-sag'-il), temple of Marduk at Babylon

Euphrates river (yu-frāt'-ēz), river bounding Mesopotamia on west

Fayum (fā-yum'), lake west of Nile

Gaumata (gau-ma'-ta), usurper of Persian throne whom Darius killed in 522

Gilgamesh (gil'-ga-mesh), early king of Uruk, hero of Mesopotamian epic

Gizeh (gē'-ze), site of great pyramids near Cairo

Gravettian culture (gra-vet'-yan), equipment of tools used in the period when Dolní Věstonice was inhabited (so named from the French site La Gravette)

Hamitic languages (ha-mit'-ik), group of languages spoken in north Africa

Hammurapi (ham-u-rap'-ē), king of Babylon 1792-1750 [formerly spelled Hammurabi]

hand-axe, large flint tool used especially for chopping meat

Hatshepsut (hat-shep'-sōōt), queen of Egypt 1490-1468

Hebrews, inhabitants of Palestine later called Jews

Herodotus (hē-rod'-ō-tus), first Greek historian about 485 to after 430

Hiram, king of Tyre about 970-940

Hittites (hit'-īts), powerful Indo-European people in Asia Minor in 2d millennium

hominid (hom'-i-nid), man-like creature (term applied especially to Australopithecines)

homo (hō'-mo), man: *erectus* (ē-rek'-tus), form of man about 400-500,000 years ago found first in Java and China; *Neanderthalensis* (nē-an-der-ta-len'-sis), form of man about 110,000-35,000 B.C.; *sapiens* (sã'-pī-enz), modern form of man from about 35,000 to present (Many other names have been given to prehistoric types of man; and even classifications are not entirely agreed. Many scholars would put Neanderthal and *homo sapiens* together.)

Horus (hō'-rus), Egyptian god of sky, also son of Osiris

Hyksos (hik'-sos), invaders of Egypt at end of Middle Kingdom

ideogram (id'-e-o-gram), written symbol expressing an idea

Imhotep (im'-ho-tep), architect of pyramid of Zoser; god of learning and doctors

Indo-European, group of languages which includes English, Greek, Persian, Sanskrit (in India), and others

Iran (ī-ran'), mountain and uplands east of Mesopotamia (modern Iran)

Isaiah (ī-zā'-ya), Hebrew prophet of 8th century; also Second Isaiah, prophet of 6th century

Ishtar (ish'-tar), Mesopotamian goddess of human fertility; also the planet Venus

Isis (ī'-sis), Egyptian goddess, wife of Osiris

Israel, northern kingdom of Hebrews, conquered by Assyria in 722

Jarmo, early agricultural site in Iraq

Jeremiah (jer-e-mī'-a), Hebrew prophet of 7th century

Jericho, early agricultural site in Jordan valley

Jerusalem, capital of Judah, site of temple of Yahweh

Judah, southern kingdom of Hebrews, conquered by Nebuchadrezzar 597-586

Karnak (kar'-nak), site of main temple to Amen

Khufu (kōō'-fōō), builder of largest of Great Pyramids about 2600

kitchen middens, banks of oyster and other shells

Leakey, Louis S. B., 1902-72, excavator in Olduvai gorge

Libby, Willard, B. 1908, discoverer of C¹⁴ method of dating organic materials

Lydia (lid'-i-a), kingdom in western Asia Minor

ma'at (ma-at'), Egyptian word for "justice"

MacNeish, R. S., Canadian archeologist who explored caves and valley of Tehuacan

Maglemosian culture (mag-le-mō'-shan), food-gathering culture in northern Europe after 10,000

Marduk (mar'-dook), patron god of Babylon

Medes, inhabitants of northern Iran who overthrew Assyrian empire in 612

meridionalis (mer-rid'-i-o-nal-is), type of elephant in early Pleistocene epoch

Mesopotamia (mes-o-po-tā'-mi-a), area between Tigris and Euphrates rivers in modern Iraq

mina (mī'-na), 1/60 of a talent, about 1 pound

Moses, Hebrew leader who made covenant with Yahweh

Mousterian (mōōs-tēr'-i-an), type of culture common in Neanderthal times

Nahum (nā'-hum), Hebrew prophet of 7th century

Naram-Sin (na-ram'-sēn), grandson of Sargon, ruler of Mesopotamia

Narmer (nar'-mer), king who united upper and lower Egypt just before 3000

Natufians (na-tu'-fi-ans), inhabitants of caves on Mount Carmel before appearance of agriculture

Neanderthal, see *homo Neanderthalensis*

Nebuchadrezzar (neb-u-kad-rez'-er), ruler of Babylonia 605-562 who destroyed temple at Jerusalem [often misspelled Nebuchadnezzar]

Nefertiti (ne-fur-tē'-tē), wife of Akhenaten

Neolithic (nē-o-lith'-ik), food-raising or "New Stone" era

Nile river, source of water and transport in Egypt

Nineveh (nin'-e-ve), capital of Assyrian empire

Nin-Khursag (nin-kōōr'-sag), Mesopotamian goddess of earth

Nippur (nip-pōōr'), sacred city of Sumerians

nome, local district of Egypt

Olduvai gorge (ōl'-du-wā), site in Tanzania with Australopithecine and later remains

Osiris (o-sī'-ris), Egyptian legendary king and god who judged the dead

paleobotanist (pā-le-o. . .), student of prehistoric plant remains

Paleolithic (pā-le-o-lith'-ik), food-gathering or "Old Stone" era

paleontologist (pā-le-on-tol'-o-jist), student of early life as preserved in bones and fossils

papyrus (pa-pī'-rus), paper made from reed plant which grows in Egypt

Persepolis (per-sep'-ō-lis), fortress-treasury in southern Persia

pharaoh (fār'-ō), title of Egyptian ruler, meaning "great house"

Phoenicia (fe-nish'-a), coastal strip south of Syria (now Lebanon)

phonogram (fō'-no-gram), written symbol expressing a phonetic value

pictogram (pik'-to-gram), written representation of physical object

Pithecanthropus, see *homo erectus*

Pleistocene (plīs'-to-sēn), first part of Cenozoic era, period of glaciers

pluvial, rainy era in southern hemisphere

Ptah (p'ta), Egyptian god worshiped especially at Memphis

Rawlinson, Henry, 1810-95, Englishman who copied Bisutun inscription

Re (rā), Egyptian god of sundisk

Samaria (sa-mar'-i-a), capital of Israel

Sargon (sar'-gon), first great imperialist, about 2371-2316

satrapy (sā'-tra-pi), province of Persian empire

Semite (sem'-īt), group of languages including Hebrew, Aramaic, Assyrian, modern Arabic

Seth, wicked brother of Osiris

Shamash (sha'-mash), Mesopotamian god of sun

Shanidar, site in Iraq where Neanderthal man lived

Shulgi (shul'-gi), Sumerian king of 3d millennium

Sin, Mesopotamian god of moon

Smerdis (smer'-dis), brother of Persian king Cambyses, who killed him; name taken by the usurper Gaumata

Solecki, Ralph S., b. 1917, excavator of Shanidar

Solomon, king of Hebrews about 965-925

Sumerians (su-mer'-i-ans), early inhabitants of Mesopotamia in first cities

Susa (sōō'-sa), a capital of Persian empire

sympathetic magic, theory that like affects like, so that charms over a representation (or part) of an animal or human being will affect the real object

taiga (tī'-ga), swampy region with coniferous forest next to but distinct from tundra

talent, weight of about 60 lb.

Tehuacan (te-wa'-kan), valley in Mexico where development of agriculture has been traced

Thebes, capital of Egypt in New Kingdom

thunder-stones, name for prehistoric flints down through 18th century

Thutmose I (tōōt-mo'-se), first Egyptian conqueror in Syria 1528-1510

Thutmose III, greatest Egyptian imperialist 1468-1436 [also spelled Thotmes and in other ways]

Tiglath-Pileser III (tig-lath-pi-lē'-zer), greatest Assyrian imperialist 744-727

Tigris river (tī'-gris), river bounding Mesopotamia on east

Tocharic (to-kar'-ik), Indo-European language spoken in central Asia

Tutankhamen (tōōt-angk-a'-men), king of Egypt 1347-1339

Tyre (tīr), major state in Phoenicia

Ugarit (u-ga'-rit), Phoenician city in 2d millennium

Uruk (u'-rūk), early city of Mesopotamia (Biblical Erech)

Ussher, James, 1581-1656, archbishop and scholar in Ireland

Ut-napishtim (ut-na-pish'-tim), character in Epic of Gilgamesh

varves, layers of earth deposited by melting glaciers

Venus figurines, small female figurines made by early *homo sapiens*

Yahweh (ya'-we), Hebrew name of God

Zagros mountains (za'-grōs), chain of mountains along eastern side of Mesopotamia

ziggurat (zig'-oo-rat), artificial mound in Mesopotamian city representing powers of earth

Zoroaster (zo-ro-as'-ter), Persian religious reformer (perhaps in early 6th century)

Zoser (zō'-ser), king of Egypt about 2700 for whom Imhotep built a step pyramid [also spelled Djoser]